December 2015

Speeches
THAT CHANGED THE WORLD

Speeches
THAT CHANGED THE WORLD

Bounty Books

First published in 2005 by Bounty Books,
a division of Octopus Publishing Group Ltd
Reprinted 2006 (twice), 2007 (four times), 2008 (three times),
2009, 2010, 2011, 2012, 2014

This edition published in 2015 by Bounty Books,
a division of Octopus Publishing Group Ltd,
Endeavour House, 189 Shaftesbury Avenue, London WC2H 8JY
www.octopusbooks.co.uk

An Hachette UK Company
www.hachette.co.uk

ISBN: 978-0-753727-71-3

A CIP catalogue record for this book is available from the British Library

Printed and bound in Malaysia

CONTENTS

INTRODUCTION

For many thousands of years, people have used oratory to influence others, but what exactly makes a speech great? Is it the choice of words, the feelings they express, the passion with which the speaker delivers them, the circumstances or the lasting effect that the speech has on what other people think or do, or even on the course of history? In fact, it can be all or any of these.

The earliest speeches that we know have, ironically, survived only because they were written down afterwards. Although they would have been heard by only a few people at the time, their influence has spread. For example, just a few soldiers would have heard Julius Caesar mutter "Alea iacta est" ("The die is cast") as he defied the Roman Senate and crossed the Rubicon into Italy with an army at his back, but that step has influenced the whole of Western history for more than 2,000 years.

The advent of mass media has had a profound effect on the influence of the spoken word: politicians are no longer trying to inspire a few people in a room, they are addressing millions via radio or television, as well as posterity. (It is chilling to think that among the first signals from Earth that might be picked up by any lurking extra terrestrials would be Adolf Hitler's broadcasts from the mid-1930s). Boris Yeltsin's speech delivered from the top of a tank outside the White House in Moscow in August 1991 was not memorable in itself, but his defiance served to prevent the Communist coup succeeding and led to the final break-up of the Soviet Union.

The speeches in *Speeches that Changed the World* are divided into ten categories: Ancient history, Love, Religion, Science, Patriotism, Philosophy, Humanity and liberty, Sport, Politics and War.
The speeches in Ancient history, Patriotism, Politics and War

inspired people to act, while those in Love, Religion, Science, Philosophy, Humanity and liberty and Sport have primarily changed the way people think or look at the world.

As well as formal speeches, several announcements and off-the-cuff remarks have also been included, because whether chilling like Stalin's "The death of one man is a tragedy, the death of millions is a statistic", the first words of an astronaut on the moon, or the announcement of a scientific break-through like the birth of Dolly the sheep, they have chronicled our history.

ANCIENT HISTORY

"THE FUNERAL ORATION OF PERICLES"

Thucydides

The historian Thucydides recorded how, in the first winter of the Peloponnesian War (431–404 BC) between Athens and rival city-state Sparta, Pericles delivered the traditional eulogy to the Athenians who had died in battle during the year. The Spartans laid siege to Athens and, although more than a quarter of the inhabitants were dead within a year, it was 27 years before the Athenians surrendered.

Most of my predecessors in this place have commended him who made this speech part of the law, telling us that it is well that it should be delivered at the burial of those who fall in battle. For myself, I should have thought that the worth which had displayed itself in deeds would be sufficiently rewarded by honours also shown by deeds; such as you now see in this funeral prepared at the people's cost. And I could have wished that the reputations of many brave men were not to be imperilled in the mouth of a single individual, to stand or fall according as he spoke well or ill. For it is hard to speak properly upon a subject where it is even difficult to convince your hearers that you are speaking the truth. On the one hand, the friend who is familiar with every fact of the story may think that some point has not been set forth with that fullness which he wishes and knows it to deserve; on the other, he who is a stranger to the matter may be led by envy to suspect exaggeration if he hears anything above his own nature. For men can endure to hear others praised only so long as they can severally persuade themselves of their own ability to equal the actions recounted: when this point is passed, envy comes in and with it incredulity. However, since our ancestors have stamped this custom with their approval, it becomes my duty to obey the law and to try to satisfy your several wishes and opinions as best I may.

I shall begin with our ancestors: it is both just and proper that they should have the honour of the first mention on an occasion like the present. They dwelt in the country without break in the succession from generation to generation, and handed it down free to the present time by their valour. And if our more remote ancestors deserve praise, much more do our own fathers, who added to their inheritance the empire which we now possess, and spared no pains to be able to leave their acquisitions to us of the present generation. Lastly, there are few parts of our dominions that have not been augmented by those of us here, who are still more or less in the vigour of life; while the mother country has been furnished by us with everything that can enable her to depend on her own resources whether for war or for peace. That part of our history which tells of the military achievements which gave us our several possessions, or of the ready valour with which either we or our fathers stemmed the tide of Hellenic or foreign aggression, is a theme too familiar to my hearers for me to dilate on, and I shall therefore pass it by. But what was the road by which we reached our position, what the form of government under which our greatness grew, what the national habits out of which it sprang; these are questions which I may try to solve before I proceed to my panegyric upon these men; since I think this to be a subject upon which on the present occasion a speaker may properly dwell, and to which the whole assemblage, whether citizens or foreigners, may listen with advantage.

Our constitution does not copy the laws of neighbouring states; we are rather a pattern to others than imitators ourselves. Its administration favours the many instead of the few; this is why it is called a democracy. If we look to the laws, they afford equal justice to all in their private differences; if not social standing, advancement in public life falls to reputation for capacity, class considerations not being allowed to interfere with merit; nor again does poverty bar the way – if a man is able to serve the state, he is not hindered by the obscurity of his condition. The freedom which we enjoy in our government extends also to our ordinary life. There, far from exercising a jealous surveillance over each other, we do not feel called upon to be angry with our neighbour for doing what he likes, or even to indulge in those injurious looks which cannot fail to be offensive, although they inflict no positive penalty. But all this ease in our private relations does not make us lawless as citizens. Against this fear is our chief safeguard, teaching us to obey the magistrates and the laws, particularly such as regard the protection of the injured, whether they are actually on the statute book, or belong to that code which, although unwritten, yet cannot be broken without acknowledged disgrace.

Further, we provide plenty of means for the mind to refresh itself from business. We celebrate games and sacrifices all the year round, and the elegance of our private establishments forms a daily source of pleasure and helps to banish the spleen; while the magnitude of our city draws the produce of the world into our harbour, so that to the Athenian the fruits of other countries are as familiar a luxury as those of his own.

If we turn to our military policy, there also we differ from our antagonists. We throw open our city to the world, and never by alien acts exclude foreigners from any opportunity of learning or observing, although the eyes of an enemy may occasionally profit by our liberality; trusting less in system and policy than in the native spirit of our citizens; while in education, where our rivals from their very cradles by a painful discipline seek after manliness, at Athens we live exactly as we please, and yet are just as ready to encounter every legitimate danger. In proof of this it may be noticed that the Lacedaemonians do not invade our country alone, but bring with them all their confederates; while we Athenians advance unsupported into the territory of a neighbour, and fighting upon a foreign soil usually vanquish with ease men who are defending their homes. Our united force was never yet encountered by any enemy, because we have at once to attend to our marine and to dispatch our citizens by land upon a hundred different services; so that, wherever they engage with some such fraction of our strength, a success against a detachment is magnified into a victory over the nation, and a defeat into a reverse suffered at the hands of our entire people. And yet if with habits not of labour but of ease, and courage not of art but of nature, we are still willing to encounter danger, we have the double advantage of escaping the experience of hardships in anticipation and of facing them in the hour of need as fearlessly as those who are never free from them.

Nor are these the only points in which our city is worthy of admiration. We cultivate refinement without extravagance and knowledge without effeminacy; wealth we employ more for use than for show, and place the real disgrace of poverty not in owning to the fact but in declining the struggle against it. Our public men have, besides politics, their private affairs to attend to, and our ordinary citizens, though occupied with the pursuits of industry, are still fair judges of public matters; for, unlike any other nation, regarding him who takes no part in these duties not as unambitious but as useless, we Athenians are able to judge at all events if we cannot originate, and, instead of looking on discussion as a stumbling-block in the way of action, we think it an indispensable preliminary to any wise action at all. Again, in our enterprises we present the singular spectacle of daring and deliberation, each carried to its highest point, and both united in the same persons; although usually decision is the fruit of ignorance, hesitation of reflection. But the palm of courage will surely be adjudged most justly to those, who best know the difference between hardship and pleasure and yet are never tempted to shrink from danger. In generosity we are equally singular, acquiring our friends by conferring, not by receiving, favours. Yet, of course, the doer of the favour is the firmer friend of the two, in order by continued kindness to keep the recipient in his debt; while the debtor feels less keenly from the very consciousness that the return he makes will be a payment, not a free gift. And it is only the Athenians, who, fearless of consequences, confer their benefits not from calculations of expediency, but in the confidence of liberality.

In short, I say that as a city we are the school of Hellas, while I doubt if the world can produce a man who, where he has only himself to depend upon, is equal to so many emergencies, and graced by so happy a versatility, as the Athenian. And that this is no mere boast thrown out for the occasion, but plain matter of fact, the power of the state acquired by these habits proves. For Athens alone of her contemporaries is found when tested to be greater than her reputation, and alone gives no occasion to her assailants to blush at the antagonist by whom they have been worsted, or to her subjects to question her title by merit to rule. Rather, the admiration of the present and succeeding ages will be ours, since we have not left our power without witness, but have shown it by mighty proofs; and far from needing a Homer for our panegyrist, or other of his craft whose verses might charm for the moment only for the impression which they gave to melt at the touch of fact, we have forced every sea and land to be the highway of our daring, and everywhere, whether for evil or for good, have left imperishable monuments behind us. Such is the Athens for which these men, in the assertion of their resolve not to lose her, nobly fought and died; and well may every one of their survivors be ready to suffer in her cause.

Indeed, if I have dwelt at some length upon the character of our country, it has been to show that our stake in the struggle is not the same as theirs who have no such blessings to lose, and also that the panegyric of the men over whom I am now speaking might be by definite proofs established. That panegyric is now in a great measure complete; for the Athens that I have celebrated is only what the heroism of these and their like have made her, men whose fame, unlike that of most Hellenes, will be found to be only commensurate with their deserts. And if a test of worth be wanted, it is to be found in their closing scene, and this not only in cases in which it set the final seal upon their merit, but also in those in which it gave the first intimation of their having any. For there is justice in the claim that steadfastness in his country's battles should be as a cloak to cover a man's other imperfections; since the good action has blotted out the bad, and his merit as a citizen more than outweighed his demerits as an individual. But none of these allowed either wealth with its prospect of future enjoyment to unnerve his spirit, or poverty with its hope of a day of freedom and riches to tempt him to shrink from danger. No, holding that vengeance upon their enemies was more to be desired than any personal blessings, and reckoning this to be the most glorious of hazards, they joyfully determined to accept the risk, to make sure of their vengeance, and to let their wishes wait; and while committing to hope the uncertainty of final success, in the business before them they thought fit to act boldly and trust in themselves. Thus choosing to die resisting, rather than to live submitting, they fled only from dishonour, but met danger face to face, and after one brief moment, while at the summit of their fortune, escaped, not from their fear, but from their glory.

So died these men as became Athenians. You, their survivors, must determine to have as unfaltering a resolution in the field, though you may pray that it may have a happier issue. And not contented with ideas derived only from words of the advantages which are bound up with the defence of your country, though these would furnish a valuable text to a speaker even before an audience so alive to them as the present, you must yourselves realize the power of Athens, and feed your eyes upon her from day to day, till love of her fills your hearts; and then, when all her greatness shall break upon you, you must reflect that it was by courage, sense of duty, and a keen feeling of honour in action that men were enabled to win all this, and that no personal failure in an enterprise could make them consent to deprive their country of their valour, but they laid it at her feet as the most glorious contribution that they could offer. For this offering of their lives made in common by them all they each of them individually received that renown which never grows old, and for a sepulchre, not so much that in which their bones have been deposited, but that noblest of shrines wherein their glory is laid up to be eternally remembered upon every occasion on which deed or story shall call for its commemoration. For heroes have the whole earth for their tomb; and in lands far from their own, where the column with its epitaph declares it, there is enshrined in every breast a record unwritten with no tablet to preserve it, except that of the heart. These take as your model and, judging happiness to be the fruit of freedom and freedom of valour, never decline the dangers of war. For it is not the miserable that would most justly be unsparing of their lives; these have nothing to hope for: it is rather they to whom continued life may bring reverses as yet unknown, and to whom a fall, if it came, would be most tremendous in its consequences. And surely, to a man of spirit, the degradation of cowardice must be immeasurably more grievous than the unfelt death which strikes him in the midst of his strength and patriotism!

Comfort, therefore, not condolence, is what I have to offer to the parents of the dead who may be here. Numberless are the chances to which, as they know, the life of man is subject; but fortunate indeed are they who draw for their lot a death so glorious as that which has caused your mourning, and to whom life has been so exactly measured as to terminate in the happiness in which it has been passed. Still I know that this is a hard saying, especially when those are in question of whom you will constantly be reminded by seeing in the homes of others blessings of which once you also boasted: for grief is felt not so much for the want of what we have never known, as for the loss of that to which we have been long accustomed. Yet you who are still of an age to beget children must bear up in the hope of having others in their stead; not only will they help you to forget those whom you have lost, but will be to the state at once a reinforcement and a security; for never can a fair or just policy be expected of the citizen who does not, like his fellows, bring to the decision the interests and apprehensions of a father. While those of you who have passed your prime must congratulate yourselves with the thought that the best part of your life was fortunate, and that the brief span that remains will be cheered by the fame of the departed. For it is only the love of honour that never grows old; and honour it is, not gain, as some would have it, that rejoices the heart of age and helplessness.

Turning to the sons or brothers of the dead, I see an arduous struggle before you. When a man is gone, all are wont to praise him, and should your merit be ever so transcendent, you will still find it difficult not merely to overtake, but even to approach their renown. The living have envy to contend with, while those who are no longer in our path are honoured with a goodwill into which rivalry does not enter. On the other hand, if I must say anything on the subject of female excellence to those of you who will now be in widowhood, it will be all comprised in this brief exhortation. Great will be your glory in not falling short of your natural character; and greatest will be hers who is least talked of among the men, whether for good or for bad.

My task is now finished. I have performed it to the best of my ability, and in word, at least, the requirements of the law are now satisfied. If deeds be in question, those who are here interred have received part of their honours already, and for the rest, their children will be brought up till manhood at the public expense: the state thus offers a valuable prize, as the garland of victory in this race of valour, for the reward both of those who have fallen and their survivors. And where the rewards for merit are greatest, there are found the best citizens.

And now that you have brought to a close your lamentations for your relatives, you may depart.

"CROSSING THE RUBICON"
Julius Caesar

In 49 BC, after years spent conquering Gaul, Julius Caesar defies Roman law and the specific orders of the controlling senate and crosses the river Rubicon back into what is now Italy, knowing that he will provoke civil war. After defeating his rival Pompey the Great at the Battle of Pharsalus in 48 BC, he becomes absolute ruler of the Roman Empire.

Alea iacta est. (The die is cast.)

"FRIENDS, ROMANS..."
Mark Antony

Although this speech has been put into Mark Antony's mouth by William Shakespeare, it is based on near-contemporary writings by Dion Cassius and Plutarch. If the conspirators' aim really had been to restore the Roman republic, their action failed. After a period of civil war, Antony, Octavian and Lepidus took control, and in 30 BC, after Antony's suicide, Octavian became uncontested ruler.

Antony: Friends, Romans, countrymen, lend me your ears;
I come to bury Caesar, not to praise him.
The evil that men do lives after them;
The good is oft interred with their bones:
So let it be with Caesar. The noble Brutus
Hath told you Caesar was ambitious:
If it were so, it was a grievous fault;
And grievously hath Caesar answer'd it.
Here, under leave of Brutus and the rest,—
For Brutus is an honourable man;
So are they all, all honorable men,—
Come I to speak in Caesar's funeral.
He was my friend, faithful and just to me:
But Brutus says he was ambitious;
And Brutus is an honourable man.
He hath brought many captives home to Rome,
Whose ransoms did the general coffers fill:
Did this in Caesar seem ambitious?
When that the poor have cried, Caesar hath wept:
Ambition should be made of sterner stuff:
Yet Brutus says he was ambitious;
And Brutus is an honourable man.
You all did see that on the Lupercal

I thrice presented him a kingly crown,
Which he did thrice refuse: was this ambition?
Yet Brutus says he was ambitious;
And, sure, he is an honourable man.
I speak not to disprove what Brutus spoke,
But here I am to speak what I do know.
You all did love him once,—not without cause:
What cause withholds you, then, to mourn for him?—
O judgment, thou art fled to brutish beasts,
And men have lost their reason!—Bear with me;
My heart is in the coffin there with Caesar,
And I must pause till it come back to me.

"THE APOLOGY OF SOCRATES"
Plato

In Athens in 399 BC, Socrates was tried, found guilty and condemned to death for corrupting his pupils by encouraging them to think. Plato made a record of the speeches the 70-year-old philosopher made in his own defence.

That I should not be grieved, O Athenians! at what has happened – namely, that you have condemned me – as well many other circumstances concur in bringing to pass; and, moreover, this, that what has happened has not happened contrary to my expectation; but I much rather wonder at the number of votes on either side. For I did not expect that I should be condemned by so small a number, but by a large majority; but now, as it seems, if only three more votes had changed sides, I should have been acquitted. So far as Melitus is concerned, as it appears to me, I have been already acquitted; and not only have I been acquitted, but it is clear to every one that had not Anytus and Lycon come forward to accuse me, he would have been fined a thousand drachmas, for not having obtained a fifth part of the votes.

The man, then, awards me the penalty of death. Well. But what shall I, on my part, O Athenians! award myself? Is it not clear that it will be such as I deserve? What, then, is that? Do I deserve to suffer, or to pay a fine? For that I have purposely during my life not remained quiet, but neglecting what most men seek after, money-making, domestic concerns, military command, popular oratory, and, moreover, all the magistracies, conspiracies, and cabals that are met with in the city, thinking that I was in reality too upright a man to be safe if I took part in such things, I therefore did not apply myself to those pursuits, by attending to which I should have been of no service either to you or to myself; but in order to confer the greatest benefit on each of you privately, as I affirm, I thereupon applied myself to that object, endeavouring to persuade every one of you not to take any care of his own affairs before he had taken care of himself in what way he may become the best and wisest, nor of the affairs of the city before he took care of the city itself; and that he should attend to other things in the same manner. What treatment, then, do I deserve, seeing I am such a man? Some reward, O Athenians! if, at least, I am to be estimated according to my real deserts; and, moreover, such a reward as would be suitable to me. What, then, is suitable to a poor man, a benefactor, and who has need of leisure in order to give you good advice? There is nothing so suitable, O Athenians! as that such a man should be maintained in the Prytaneum, and this much more than if one of you had been victorious at the Olympic games in a horserace, or in the two- or four-horsed chariot race: for such a one makes you appear to be happy, but I, to be so; and he does not need support, but I do. If, therefore, I must award a sentence according to my just deserts, I award this, maintenance in the Prytaneum.

Perhaps, however, in speaking to you thus, I appear to you to speak in the same presumptuous manner as I did respecting commiseration and entreaties; but such is not the case, O Athenians! it is rather this: I am persuaded that I never designedly injured any man, though I can not persuade you of this, for we have conversed with each other but for a short time. For if there were the same law with you as with other men, that in capital cases the trial should list not only one day, but many, I think you would be persuaded; but it is not easy in a short time to do away with great calumnies. Being persuaded, then, that I have injured no one, I am far from intending to injure myself, and from pronouncing against myself that I am deserving of punishment, and from awarding myself anything of the kind. Through fear of what? Lest I should suffer that which Melitus awards me, of which I say I know not whether it be good or evil. Instead of this, shall I choose what I well know to be evil, and award that? Shall I choose imprisonment? And why should I live in prison, a slave to the established magistracy, the Eleven? Shall I choose a fine, and to be imprisoned until I have paid it? But this is the same as that which I just now mentioned, for I have not money to pay it. Shall I, then, award myself exile? For perhaps you would consent to this award. I should indeed be very fond of life, O Athenians! if I were so devoid of reason as not to be able to reflect that you, who are my fellow-citizens, have been unable to endure my manner of life and discourses, but they have become so burdensome and odious to you that you now seek to be rid of them: others, however, will easily bear them. Far from it, O Athenians! A fine life it would be for me at my age to go out wandering, and driven from city to city, and so to live. For I well know that, wherever I may go, the youth will listen to me when I speak, as they do here. And if I repulse them, they will themselves drive me out, persuading the elders; and if I do not repulse them, their fathers and kindred will banish me on their account.

Perhaps, however, someone will say, "Can you not, Socrates, when you have gone from us, live a silent and quiet life?" This is the most difficult thing of all to persuade some of you. For if I say that that would be to disobey the deity, and that, therefore, it is impossible for me to live quietly, you would not believe me, thinking I spoke ironically. If, on the other hand, I say that this is the greatest good to man, to discourse daily on virtue, and other things which you have heard me discussing, examining both myself and others, but that a life without investigation is not worth living, still less would you believe me if I said this. Such, however, is the case, as I affirm, O Athenians! though it is not easy to persuade you. And at the same time I am not accustomed to think myself deserving of any ill. If, indeed, I were rich, I would amerce myself in such a sum as I should be able to pay; for then I should have suffered no harm, but now – for I cannot, unless you are willing to amerce me in such a sum as I am able to pay. But perhaps I could pay you a mina of silver: in that sum, then, I amerce myself. But Plato here, O Athenians! and Crito Critobulus and Apollodorus bid me amerce myself in thirty minae, and they offer to be sureties. I amerce myself, then, to you in that sum; and they will be sufficient sureties for the money.

The judges now proceeded to pass the sentence, and condemned Socrates to death; whereupon he continued.

For the sake of no long space of time, O Athenians! you will incur the character and reproach at the hands of those who wish to defame the city, of having put that wise man, Socrates, to death. For those who wish to defame you will assert that I am wise, though I am not. If, then, you had waited for a short time, this would have happened of its own accord; for observe my age, that it is far advanced in life, and near death. But I say this not to you all, but to those only who have condemned me to die. And I say this, too, to the same persons. Perhaps you think, O Athenians! that I have been convicted through the want of arguments, by which I might have persuaded you, had I thought it right to do and say anything, so that I might escape punishment. Far otherwise: I have been convicted through want indeed, yet not of arguments, but of audacity and impudence, and of the inclination to say such things to you as would have been most agreeable for you to hear, had I lamented and bewailed and done and said many other things unworthy of me, as I affirm, but such as you are accustomed to hear from others. But neither did I then think that I ought, for the sake of avoiding danger, to do anything unworthy of a freeman, nor do I now repent of having so defended myself; but I should much rather choose to die, having so defended myself, than to live in that way. For neither in a trial nor in battle is it right that I or anyone else should employ every possible means whereby he may avoid death; for in battle it is frequently evident that a man might escape death by laying down his arms, and throwing himself on the mercy of his pursuers. And there are many other devices in every danger, by which to avoid death, if a man dares to do and say everything. But this is not difficult, O Athenians! to escape death; but it is much more difficult to avoid depravity, for it runs swifter than death. And now I, being slow and aged, am overtaken by the slower of the two; but my accusers, being strong and active, have been overtaken by the swifter, wickedness. And now I depart, condemned by you to death; but they condemned by truth, as guilty of iniquity and injustice: and I abide my sentence, and so do they. These things, perhaps, ought so to be, and I think that they are for the best.

In the next place, I desire to predict to you who have condemned me, what will be your fate; for I am now in that condition in which men most frequently prophesy – namely, when they are about to die. I say, then, to you, O Athenians! who have condemned me to death, that immediately after my death a punishment will overtake you, far more severe, by Jupiter! than that which you have inflicted on me. For you have done this, thinking you should be freed from the necessity of giving an account of your lives. The very contrary, however, as I affirm, will happen to you. Your accusers will be more numerous, whom I have now restrained, though you did not perceive it; and they will be more severe, inasmuch as they are younger, and you will be more indignant. For if you think that by putting men to death you will restrain anyone from upbraiding you because you do not live well, you are much mistaken; for this method of escape is neither possible nor honorable; but that other is most honorable and most easy, not to put a check upon others, but for a man to take heed to himself how he may be most perfect. Having predicted thus much to those of you who have condemned me, I take my leave of you.

But with you who have voted for my acquittal I would gladly hold converse on what has now taken place, while the magistrates are busy, and I am not yet carried to the place where I must die. Stay with me, then, so long, O Athenians! for nothing hinders our conversing with each other, while we are permitted to do so; for I wish to make known to you, as being my friends, the meaning of that which has just now befallen me. To me, then, O my judges! – and in calling you judges I call you rightly – a strange thing has happened. For the wonted prophetic voice of my guardian deity on every former occasion, even in the most trifling affairs, opposed me if I was about to do anything wrong; but now that has befallen me which ye yourselves behold, and which anyone would think, and which is supposed to be the extremity of evil; yet neither when I departed from home in the morning did the warning of the god oppose me, nor when I came up here to the place of trial, nor in my address when I was about to say anything; yet on other occasions it has frequently restrained me in the midst of speaking. But now it has never, throughout this proceeding, opposed me, either in what I did or said. What, then, do I suppose to be the cause of this? I will tell you: what has befallen me appears to be a blessing; and it is impossible that we think rightly who suppose that death is an evil. A great proof of this to me is the fact that it is impossible but that the accustomed signal should have opposed me, unless I had been about to meet with some good.

Moreover, we may hence conclude that there is great hope that death is a blessing. For to die is one of two things: for either the dead may be annihilated, and have no sensation of anything whatever; or, as it is said, there are a certain change and passage of the soul from one place to another. And if it is a privation of all sensation, as it were a sleep in which the sleeper has no dream, death would be a wonderful gain. For I think that if anyone, having selected a night in which he slept so soundly as not to have had a dream, and having compared this night with all the other nights and days of his life, should be required, on consideration, to say how many days and nights he had passed better and more pleasantly than this night throughout his life, I think that not only a private person but even the great king himself would find them easy to number, in comparison with other days and nights. If, therefore, death is a thing of this kind, I say it is a gain; for thus all futurity appears to be nothing more than one night. But if, on the other hand, death is a removal from hence to another place, and what is said be true, that all the dead are there, what greater blessing can there be than this, my judges? For if, on arriving at Hades, released from these who pretend to be judges, one shall find those who are true judges, and who are said to judge there, Minos and Rhadamanthus, Facus and Triptolemus, and such others of the demi-gods as were just during their own life, would this be a sad removal? At what price would you not estimate a conference with Orpheus and Musëus, Hesiod and Homer? I indeed should be willing to die often, if this be true. For to me the sojourn there would be admirable, when I should meet with Palamedes, and Ajax, son of Telamon, and any other of the ancients who has died by an unjust sentence. The comparing my sufferings with theirs would, I think, be no unpleasing occupation. But the greatest pleasure would be to spend my time in questioning and examining the people there as I have done those here, and discovering who among them is wise, and who fancies himself to be so, but is not. At what price, my judges, would not anyone estimate the opportunity of questioning him who led that mighty army against Troy, or Ulysses, or Sisyphus, or ten thousand others whom one might mention both men and women – with whom to converse and associate, and to question them, would be an inconceivable happiness? Surely for that the judges there do not condemn to death; for in other respects those who live there are more happy than those who are here, and are henceforth immortal, if, at least, what is said be true.

You, therefore, O my judges! ought to entertain good hopes with respect to death, and to meditate on this one truth, that to a good man nothing is evil, neither while living nor when dead, nor are his concerns neglected by the gods. And what has befallen me is not the effect of chance; but this is clear to me, that now to die, and be freed from my cares is better for me. On this account the warning in no way turned me aside; and I bear no resentment toward those who condemned me, or against my accusers, although they did not condemn and accuse me with this intention, but thinking to injure me: in this they deserve to be blamed.

Thus much, however, I beg of them. Punish my sons when they grow up, O judges! paining them as I have pained you, if they appear to you to care for riches or anything else before virtue; and if they think themselves to be something when they are nothing, reproach them as I have done you, for not attending to what they ought, and for conceiving themselves to be something when they are worth nothing. If ye do this, both I and my sons shall have met with just treatment at your hands.

But it is now time to depart – for me to die, for you to live. But which of us is going to a better state is unknown to everyone but God.

"COMMON CAUSE WITH THE PEOPLE"
Demosthenes

Demosthenes is widely regarded as the best orator in the ancient world. Greece was under threat from the expansionist Philip of Macedonia and Demosthenes made a series of speeches urging his compatriots to unite and preserve their freedom. His efforts failed and Athens lost the war. Aeschines, another powerful political figure and member of the embassy, who had signed the peace treaty with Philip, accused Demosthenes of taking a bribe. The following extracts are taken from his trial in 330 BC, in which he compared his life and his conduct with those of Aeschines. His oratory won the day and Aeschines was forced into exile.

It was my lot, Aeschines, when a boy, to frequent the schools suited to my station, and to have wherewithal to avoid doing anything mean through want. When I emerged from boyhood, I did as was consistent with my origin; filled the office of Choregus, furnished galleys, contributed to the revenue, and was wanting in no acts of munificence, public or private, but ready to aid both my country and my friends. When I entered into public life, I deemed it proper to choose the course which led to my being repeatedly crowned both by this country and the other Greek states, so that not even you, my enemies, will now venture to pronounce the part I took other than honourable. Such then were my fortunes...

But you, venerable man, who look down upon others, see what kind of fortunes were yours compared with mine! Brought up from your boyhood in abject poverty, you both were helper in your father's school, and you ground the ink, sponged the forms and swept the room, doing the work of a household slave, not of a freeborn youth. When grown up, you recited your mother's books as she performed her mysteries, and you helped in her other trickeries. At night, dressed like a bacchanal, and draining the goblet, and purifying the initiated, and rubbing them with clay and with bran, rising from the lustration, you ordered them to cry, "I've fled the evil; I've found the good"; bragging that none ever roared so loud before; and truly I believe it; for do not doubt that he who now speaks out so lustily, did not then howl most splendidly...

I come to the charges that apply to your life and conversation. You chose that line of policy (ever since the plan struck your mind) by which, as long as the country flourished, you led the life of the hare, frightened and trembling, and perpetually expecting the scourge for the offences of which you were conscious; but when all others were suffering, you were seen in high spirits by all. But he who was so cheerful after the death of thousands of his fellow-citizens, what does he deserve to suffer at the hands of the survivors?...

Draw then the parallel between your life and mine, Aeschines, quietly and not acrimoniously; and demand of this audience which of the two each of them had rather choose for his own...your measures were all in the enemy's favour – mine always in the country's; and, in a word, now on this day the question as to me is whether or not I shall be crowned, while nothing whatever is alleged against my integrity; while it is your lot to appear already as a calumniator, and the choice of evils before you is that of still continuing your trade, or being put to silence by failing to obtain a fifth of the votes...

Does anyone wilfully do wrong? He is the object of indignation and punishment. Does anyone commit an error unintentionally? He is pardoned, not punished. Has one who neither does any wrong nor commits any error devoted himself to a course which to all appeared expedient, and has he been in common with all disappointed of success? It is not fair to reprobate or to attack him, but to condole with him...Thus has Aeschines so far surpassed all other men in cruelty and calumny, that those same things which he enumerates as misfortunes he also imputes to me as crimes...

In what circumstances then ought a statesman and an orator to be vehement? When the state is in jeopardy upon the ruin of affairs – when the people are in conflict with the enemy – then it is that the strenuous and patriotic citizen appears. But when Aeschines cannot pretend to have any ground whatever for even charging me with any offence in public life, or, I will add, in private, either in the name of the country or his own – for him to come forward with a vamped-up attack on my crowning and my honours, and to waste so many words upon this subject, is the working of personal spite and envy and a little mind, and shows no good man.

To me, indeed, Aeschines, it appears from these speeches of yours, as if you had instituted this impeachment through a desire of making a display of vociferation, not of punishing anyone's misconduct. For it is not the speech of the orator, Aeschines, that avails, nor yet the compass of his voice, but his feeling in unison with the comunity and bearing enmity or affection towards them whom his country loves or hates. He that possesses his soul speaks ever with right feeling. But he that bows to those from whom the country has danger to apprehend, does not anchor in the same roadstead with the people; accordingly he does not look for safety from the same quarter. But, mark me, I do: for I have always made common cause with the people, nor have I ever taken any course for my peculiar and individual interest. Can you say as much? Then how? – You, who, instantly after the battle, went on the embassy to Philip, the cause of all that in these times befell your country; and that after refusing the office at all former periods, as everyone knows? – But who deceives the country? Is it not he that says one thing and thinks another? And who is he upon whom at every assembly solemn execration is proclaimed? Is it not such a man as this? What worse charge can anyone bring against an orator than that his words and his sentiments do not tally? Yet you have been discovered to be such a man; and you still lift your voice and dare to look this assembly in the face!...

What alliance ever accrued to the country of your making? Or what succours, or goodwill, or glory of your gaining? Or what embassy, or what other public functions, whereby the state acquired honour? What domestic affair, or concern of the Greek states, or of strangers, over which you presided, was ever set right through you? What galleys, what armaments, what arsenals, what repairs of the walls, what cavalry? In what one of all these particulars have you ever proved useful? What benefit has ever accrued to either rich or poor from your fortunes? None. "But, hark!" says someone, "if nothing of all this was done, at least there existed good dispositions and public spirit." Where? When? You most wicked of men – your contributing nothing was not owing to your poverty but to your taking special care that nothing you did should ever counteract the schemes of those to whom all your policy was subservient. In what, then, are you bold, and when are you munificent? When anything is to be urged against your countrymen, then are you most copious of speech – most profuse of money – most rich in memory – a first-rate actor – the Theocrines of the stage!...

Two qualities, men of Athens, every citizen of ordinary worth ought to possess...he should both maintain in office the purpose of a firm mind and the course suited to his country's pre-eminence, and on all occasions and in all his actions the spirit of patriotism. This belongs to our nature; victory and might are under the dominion of another power. These dispositions you will find to have been absolutely inherent in me. For observe; neither when my head was demanded, nor when they dragged me before the Amphyctions, nor when they threatened, nor when they promised, nor when they let loose on me these wretches like wild beasts, did I ever abate in any particular my affection for you. This straightforward and honest path of policy, from the very first, I chose; the honour, the power, the glory of my country to promote – these to augment – in these to have my being. Never was I seen going about the streets elated and exulting when the enemy was victorious, stretching out my hand, and congratulating such as I thought would tell it elsewhere, but hearing with alarm any success of our own armies, moaning and bent to the earth like these impious men, who rail at this country as if they could do so without stigmatizing themselves; and who, turning their eyes abroad, and seeing the prosperity of the enemy in the calamities of

Greece, rejoice in them, and maintain that we should labour to make them last for ever!

Let not, oh gracious God, let not such conduct receive any manner of sanction from thee! Rather plant even in these men a better spirit and better feelings! But if they are wholly incurable, then pursue themselves, yea, themselves by themselves, to utter and untimely perdition by land and by sea; and to us who are spared vouchsafe to grant the speediest rescue from our impending alarms, and an unshaken security!

LOVE

"AT THE CENTRE OF NONVIOLENCE STANDS THE PRINCIPLE OF LOVE"
Martin Luther King Jr

In the 1960s, the United States was a highly segregated society, with widespread legalized discrimination on the grounds of race. Dr Martin Luther King was influenced by Mahatma Gandhi's ideas on nonviolence as a means to achieve change and attain civil rights.

Nonviolent resistance avoids not only external physical violence but also internal violence of spirit. At the centre of nonviolence stands the principle of love. In struggling for human dignity the oppressed people of the world must not allow themselves to become bitter or indulge in hate campaigns. To retaliate with hate and bitterness would do nothing but intensify the hate in the world. Along the way of life, someone must have sense enough and morality enough to cut off the chain of hate. This can be done only by projecting the ethics of love to the centre of our lives.

"WHATEVER LOVE MEANS"
Charles, Prince of Wales

During the press conference after the announcement of their engagement on February 24, 1981, one journalist asked the couple whether they were in love. When asked the question: "Are you in love?" Diana said, "Of course." Charles replied that he was too, but added:

Whatever love means.

"...THERE WERE THREE OF US IN THIS MARRIAGE"
Diana, Princess of Wales

In November 1995, Princess Diana was interviewed by the journalist Martin Bashir for the BBC's current affairs programme, *Panorama*. Among other subjects she discussed her marriage, her relationship with her husband's family, her bulimia, her relationship with the British public and press and her own infidelity. The following was part of the discussion about her realization that her husband still had a close relationship with his ex-mistress.

Well, there were three of us in this marriage, so it was a bit crowded.

"THE ABDICATION SPEECH"
Edward VIII

On January 20, 1936, the Prince of Wales succeeded his father, George V, as king. His relationship with Mrs Wallis Simpson had been causing an increasing scandal, and her divorce in November of the same year provoked a constitutional crisis as the government felt that the public would not accept her as queen. The instrument of abdication was executed on 10 December, and on the following day the former king made his decision known across the empire in this broadcast.

At long last I am able to say a few words of my own. I have never wanted to withhold anything, but until now it has not been constitutionally possible for me to speak.

A few hours ago I discharged my last duty as King and Emperor, and now that I have been succeeded by my brother, The Duke of York, my first words must be to declare my allegiance to him. This I do with all my heart.

You all know the reasons which have impelled me to renounce the throne. But I want you to understand that in making up my mind I did not forget the country or the Empire which as Prince of Wales, and lately as King, I have for twenty-five years tried to serve. But you must believe me when I tell you that I have found it impossible to carry the heavy burden of responsibility and to discharge my duties as King as I would wish to do without the help and support of the woman I love.

And I want you to know that the decision I have made has been mine and mine alone. This was a thing I had to judge entirely for myself. The other person most nearly concerned has tried up to the last to persuade me to take a different course. I have made this, the most serious decision of my life, only upon the single thought of what would in the end be best for all.

This decision has been made less difficult to me by the sure knowledge that my brother, with his long training in the public affairs of this country and with his fine qualities, will be able to take my place forthwith, without interruption or injury to the life and progress of the Empire. And he has one matchless blessing, enjoyed by so many of you and not bestowed on me – a happy home with his wife and children.

During these hard days I have been comforted by Her Majesty my mother and by my family. The Ministers of the Crown, and in particular Mr Baldwin, the Prime Minister, have always treated me with full consideration. There has never been any constitutional difference between me and them and between me and Parliament. Bred in the constitutional tradition by my father, I should never have allowed any such issue to arise.

Ever since I was Prince of Wales, and later on when I occupied the Throne, I have been treated with the greatest kindness by all classes of the people, wherever I have lived or journeyed throughout the Empire. For that I am very grateful.

I now quit altogether public affairs, and I lay down my burden. It may be some time before I return to my native land, but I shall always follow the fortunes of the British race and Empire with profound interest, and if at any time in the future I can be found of service to His Majesty in a private station I shall not fail.

And now we all have a new King. I wish him, and you, his people, happiness and prosperity with all my heart. God bless you all. God Save The King.

"...I DID HAVE A RELATIONSHIP WITH MS LEWINSKY..."
Bill Clinton

On August 17, 1998 President Clinton of the USA made the following speech. The independent counsel referred to is the Republican lawyer Kenneth Starr, whom many saw as having political motives for hounding the President over allegations of inappropriate behaviour with both Monica Lewinsky and Paula Jones, and particularly over the Whitewater financial scandal. The muck-raking that appeared in the press, although unfounded or even manufactured, damaged the Clinton presidency and may have been instrumental in the return of the Republicans to the White House in January 2000.

This afternoon in this room, from this chair, I testified before the Office of Independent Counsel and the Grand Jury. I answered their questions truthfully, including questions about my private life, questions no American citizen would ever want to answer. Still, I must take complete responsibility for all my actions, both public and private. And that is why I am speaking to you tonight.

As you know, in a deposition in January, I was asked questions about my relationship with Monica Lewinsky. While my answers were legally accurate, I did not volunteer information. Indeed, I did have a relationship with Ms Lewinsky that was not appropriate. In fact, it was wrong. It constituted a critical lapse in judgment and a personal failure on my part for which I am solely and completely responsible.

But I told the Grand Jury today and I say to you now that at no time did I ask anyone to lie, to hide or destroy evidence, or to take any other unlawful action. I know that my public comments and my silence about this matter gave a false impression. I misled people, including even my wife. I deeply regret that. I can only tell you I was motivated by many factors. First by a desire to protect myself from the embarrassment of my own conduct. I was also very concerned about protecting my family. The fact that these questions were being asked in a politically inspired lawsuit, which has since been dismissed, was a consideration, too.

In addition, I had real and serious concerns about an independent counsel investigation that began with private business dealings twenty years ago, dealings, I might add, about which an independent federal agency found no evidence of any wrongdoing by me or my wife over two years ago. The independent counsel investigation moved on to my staff and friends, then into my private life. And now the investigation itself is under investigation. This has gone on too long, cost too much and hurt too many innocent people.

Now this matter is between me, the two people I love most – my wife and our daughter – and our God. I must put it right, and I am prepared to do whatever it takes to do so. Nothing is more important to me personally. But it is private, and I intend to reclaim my family life for my family. It's nobody's business but ours.

Even presidents have private lives. It's time to stop the pursuit of personal destruction and the prying into private lives and get on with our national life. Our country has been distracted by this matter for too long, and I take my responsibility for my part in all this. That is all I can do. Now it is time – in fact, it is past time – to move on. We have important work to do, real opportunities to seize, real problems to solve, real security matters to face.

And so, tonight, I ask you to turn away from the spectacle of the past seven months, to repair the fabric of our national discourse and to return our attention to all the challenges and all the promise of the next American century. Thank you for watching. And good night.

"THE BEDROOMS OF THE NATION"

In 1967, Justice Minister Pierre Elliot Trudeau (who later became Canada's Prime Minister) was responsible for removing laws against homosexuality from the Criminal Code of Canada, famously remarking:

The state has no business in the bedrooms of the nation.

"DEFINITION OF LOVE"
St Paul

In I Corinthians 13: 4–7, St Paul defines Christian love.

Love is patient and kind. Love knows neither envy nor jealousy. Love is not forward and self-assertive, nor boastful and conceited.

She does not behave unbecomingly, nor seek to aggrandize herself, nor blaze out in passionate anger, nor brood over wrongs.

She finds no pleasure in injustice done to others, but joyfully sides with the truth.

She knows how to be silent. She is full of trust, full of hope, full of patient endurance.

"GOD'S LOVE TO FALLEN MAN"
John Wesley

The 18th-century evangelical John Wesley led a great revival of Christianity in England. Banned from churches because of his hectoring and very long sermons, he preached in fields to crowds of up to 30,000 people. The following passages are taken from a far longer sermon on the subject of divine love and salvation.

"Not as the offence, so also is the free gift." Romans 5:15.
How exceeding common, and how bitter, is the outcry against our first parent for the mischief which he not only brought upon himself, but entailed upon his latest posterity! It was by his wilful rebellion against God that "sin entered into the world". "By one man's disobedience", as the Apostle observes, the many, *hoi polloi,* as many as were then in the loins of their forefather, "were made", or constituted, "sinners": Not only deprived of the favour of God, but also of this image, of all virtue, righteousness, and true holiness; and sunk, partly into the image of the devil, – in pride, malice, and all other diabolical tempers; partly into the image of the brute, being fallen under the dominion of brutal passions and grovelling appetites. Hence also death entered into the world, with all his forerunners and attendants, – pain, sickness, and a whole train of uneasy, as well as unholy passions and tempers.

"For all this we may thank Adam," has echoed down from generation to generation...Has not your heart, and probably your lips too, joined in the general charge?

Nay it were well if the charge rested here: But it is certain it does not...Some, indeed, have done this a little more modestly, in an oblique and indirect manner; but others have thrown aside the mask, and asked, "Did not God foresee that Adam would abuse his liberty? And did he not know the baneful consequences which this must naturally have on all his posterity? And why, then, did he permit that disobedience? Was it not easy for the Almighty to have prevented it?" – He certainly did foresee the whole...But it was known to him, at the same time, that it was best, upon the whole, not to prevent it. He knew that...the evil resulting from the former was not as the good resulting from the latter, – not worthy to be compared with it. He saw that to permit the fall of the first man was far best for mankind in general; that abundantly more good than evil would accrue to the posterity of Adam by his fall; that if "sin abounded" thereby over all the earth, yet grace "would much more abound"; yea, and that to every individual of the human race, unless it was his own choice...

...Mankind in general have gained, by the fall of Adam, a capacity of attaining more holiness and happiness on earth than it would have been possible for them to attain if Adam had not fallen. For if Adam had not fallen, Christ had not died. Nothing can be more clear than this; nothing more undeniable. Unless all the partakers of human nature had received that deadly wound in Adam, it would not have been needful for the Son of God to take our nature upon him...there would have been no room for that amazing display of the Son of God's love to mankind...It could not then have been said, to the astonishment of all the hosts of heaven "God so loved the world that he gave his Son" out of his bosom, his only-begotten Son, "to the end that whosoever believeth on him should not perish, but have everlasting life."

...What is the necessary consequence of this? It is this: There could then have been no such thing as faith in God thus loving the world, giving his only Son for us men, and for our salvation...the whole privilege of justification by faith could have had no existence; there could have been no redemption in the blood of Christ; neither could Christ have been "made of God unto us", either "wisdom, righteousness. sanctification" or "redemption".

We see then, what unspeakable advantage we derive from the fall of our first parent with regard to faith; -- Faith both in God the Father, who spared not his own Son, his only Son, but "wounded him for our transgressions", and "bruised him for our iniquities": and in God the Son, who poured out his soul for us transgressors, and washed us in his own blood. We see what advantage we derive therefrom with regard to the love of God; both of God the Father and God the Son. The chief ground of this love, as long as we remain in the body, is plainly declared by the Apostle: "We love Him, because He first loved us." But the greatest instance of his love had never been given, if Adam had not fallen.

And as our faith both in God the Father and the Son, receives an unspeakable increase, if not its very being, from this grand event, as does also our love both of the Father and the Son; so does the love of our neighbour also, our benevolence to all mankind, which cannot but increase in the same proportion with our faith and love of God. For who does not apprehend the force of that inference drawn by the loving Apostle: "Beloved, if God so loved us, we ought also to love one another"? If God SO loved us, – observe, the stress of the argument lies on this very point: SO loved us, as to deliver up his only Son to die a cursed death for our salvation. Beloved, what manner of love is this wherewith God hath loved us; so as to give his only Son, in glory equal with the Father, in Majesty co-eternal? What manner of love is this wherewith the only-begotten Son of God hath loved us so as to empty himself, as far as possible, of his eternal Godhead; as to divest himself of that glory which he had with the Father before the world began; as to take upon him the form of a servant, being found in fashion as a man; and then, to humble himself still further, "being obedient unto death, even the death of the cross!" If God SO loved us, how ought we to love one another! But this motive to brotherly love had been totally wanting if Adam had not fallen. Consequently, we could not then have loved one another in so high a degree as we may now. Nor could there have been that height and depth in the command of our blessed Lord, "As I have loved you, So love one another."

"GREATER LOVE HATH NO MAN"
Jesus Christ

A short time before his arrest, towards the end of the Last Supper, Jesus gave the following instructions to his apostles (John 15: 9–17)

9 As the Father hath loved me, so have I loved you: continue ye in
my love.
10 If ye keep my commandments, ye shall abide in my love; even
as I have kept my Father's commandments, and abide in his love.
11 These things have I spoken unto you, that my joy might remain
in you, and that your joy might be full.
12 This is my commandment, That ye love one another, as I have
loved you.
13 Greater love hath no man than this, that a man lay down his life
for his friends.
14 Ye are my friends, if ye do whatsoever I command you.
15 Henceforth I call you not servants; for the servant knoweth not
what his lord doeth: but I have called you friends; for all things
that I have heard of my Father I have made known unto you.
16 Ye have not chosen me, but I have chosen you, and ordained
you, that ye should go and bring forth fruit, and that your fruit
should remain: that whatsoever ye shall ask of the Father in my
name, he may give it you.
17 These things I command you, that ye love one another.

‘THE LOVE OF A DOG”
George Graham Vest

George Graham Vest was Senator for Missouri from 1879 to 1903 and one of the leading orators of his time. Earlier, when he practised law, he gave this speech in court while representing a man who was suing another for killing his dog. Vest ignored the testimony and concentrated on the loyalty of dogs, so being an early exponent of the art of appealing to the emotions of the jury rather than letting the facts get in the way.

Gentlemen of the Jury: The best friend a man has in the world may turn against him and become his enemy. His son or daughter that he has reared with loving care may prove ungrateful. Those who are nearest and dearest to us, those whom we trust with our happiness and our good name, may become traitors to their faith. The money that a man has, he may lose. It flies away from him, perhaps when he needs it most. A man's reputation may be sacrificed in a moment of ill-considered action. The people who are prone to fall on their knees to do us honour when success is with us may be the first to throw the stone of malice when failure settles its cloud upon our heads.

The one absolutely unselfish friend that man can have in this selfish world, the one that never deserts him, the one that never proves ungrateful or treacherous, is his dog. A man's dog stands by him in prosperity and in poverty, in health and in sickness. He will sleep on the cold ground, where the wintry winds blow and the snow drives fiercely, if only he may be near his master's side. He will kiss the hand that has no food to offer. He will lick the wounds and sores that come in encounters with the roughness of the world. He guards the sleep of his pauper master as if he were a prince. When all other friends desert, he remains. When riches take wings, and reputation falls to pieces, he is as constant in his love as the sun in its journey through the heavens. If fortune drives the master forth, an outcast in the world, friendless and homeless, the faithful dog asks no higher privilege than that of accompanying him, to guard him against danger, to fight against his enemies. And when the last scene of all comes, and death takes his master in its embrace and his body is laid away in the cold ground, no matter if all other friends pursue their way, there by the graveside will the noble dog be found, his head between his paws, his eyes sad, but open in alert watchfulness, faithful and true even in death.

"THE GOLDEN SPEECH"
Elizabeth I

On November 30, 1601, at the age of 68, Elizabeth made what was to be her last speech to her parliament. Although the country as a whole was more prosperous than at the beginning of her reign, the monarchy was continually in financial straits and shortly before parliament had forced her to surrender lucrative monopolies that she had given to favourites. This speech is not just a glorious reiteration of her love for her people, but also a furious denial of public accusations of graft.

To her last parliament
The 30 of November 1601; her Majestie being sat under State in the Council Chamber at Whitehall, the Speaker, accompanied with

Privy Councillors, besides Knights and Burgesses of the lower House to the number of eight-score, presenting themselves at her Majesty's feet, for that so graciously and speedily she had heard and yielded to her Subjects' desires, and proclaimed the same in their hearing as followeth.

Mr Speaker,
We perceive your coming is to present thanks unto Us; Know I accept them with no less joy than your loves can have desire to offer such a Present, and do more esteem it than any Treasure of Riches, for those We know how to prize, but Loyalty, Love, and Thanks, I account them invaluable, and though God hath raised Me high, yet this I account the glory of my Crown, that I have reigned with your Loves. This makes that I do not so much rejoice that God hath made Me to be a Queen, as to be a Queen over so thankful a People, and to be the mean under God to conserve you in safety, and preserve you from danger, yea to be the Instrument to deliver you from dishonour, from shame, and from infamy; to keep you from out of servitude, and from slavery under our Enemies; and cruel tyranny, and vile oppression intended against Us: for the better withstanding wherof, We take very acceptably your intended helps, and chiefly in that it manifesteth your loves and largeness of heart to your Sovereign. Of My self I must say this, I never was any greedy scraping grasper, nor a strict fast holding Prince, nor yet a waster. My heart was never set upon any worldly goods, but only for my Subjects' good. What you do bestow on Me, I will not hoard up, but receive it to bestow on you again; yea Mine own Properties I account yours to be expended for your good, and your eyes shall see the bestowing of it for your welfare.

Mr Speaker, I would wish you and the rest to stand up, for I fear I shall yet trouble you with longer speech.

Mr Speaker, you give me thanks, but I am more to thank you, and I charge you, thank them of the Lower House from Me, for had I not received knowledge from you, I might have fallen into the lapse of an Error, only for want of true information.

Since I was Queen yet did I never put my pen to any grant but upon pretext and semblance made Me, that it was for the good and avail of my Subjects generally, though a private profit to some of my ancient servants who had deserved well: But that my Grants shall be made Grievances to my People, and Oppressions, to be privileged under colour of Our Patents, Our Princely Dignity shall not suffer it.

When I heard it, I could give no rest unto my thoughts until I had reformed it, and those Varlets, lewd persons, abusers of my bounty, shall know I will not suffer it. And Mr Speaker, tell the House from me, I take it exceeding grateful, that the knowledge of these things are come unto me from them. And though amongst them the principal Members are such as are not touched in private, and therefore need not speak from any feeling of the grief, yet We have heard that other Gentlemen also of the House, who stand as free, have spoken as freely in it, which gives Us to know that no respects or interests have moved them other then the minds they beare to suffer no diminution of our Honour, and our Subjects' love unto Us. The zeal of which affection tending to ease my People, and knit their hearts unto us, I embrace with a Princely care far above all earthly Treasures. I esteem my People's love, more than which I desire not to merit: And God that gave me here to sit, and placed me over you, knows that I never respected my self, but as your good was conserved in me; yet what dangers, what practices, and what perils I have passed, some, if not all of you know: but none of these things do move me, or ever made me feare but it is God that hath delivered me.

And in my governing this Land, I have ever set the last Judgement day before mine eyes, and so to rule, as I shall be Judged and answer before a higher Judge, to whose Judgement Seat I do appeal in that never thought was cherished in my heart that tended not to my People's good.

And if my Princely bounty have been abused, and my Grants

turned to the hurt of my People contrary to my will and meaning, or if any in Authority under me have neglected or converted what I have committed unto them, I hope God they will not lay their culps to my charge.

To be a King, and wear a Crown, is a thing more glorious to them that see it, than it is pleasant to them that bear it: for my self, I never was so much inticed with the glorious name of a King, or the royal authority of a Queen, as delighted that God hath made me His Instrument to maintain His Truth and Glory, and to defend this Kingdom from dishonour, damage, tyranny, and oppression; But should I ascribe any of these things unto my self, or my sexly weakness, I were not worthy to live, and of all most unworthy of the mercies I have received at God's hands but to God only and wholly all is given and ascribed.

The cares and trouble of a Crown I cannnot more fitly resemble than to the drugs of a learned Physician, perfumed with some aromatical savour, or to bitter pills gilded over, by which they are made more acceptable or less offensive, which indeed are bitter and unpleasant to take; and for my own part, were it not for Conscience sake to discharge the duty that God hath laid upon me, and to maintain his glory, and keep you in safety; in mine own disposition I should be willing to resign the place I hold to any other, and glad to be freed of the Glory with the Labours, for it is not my desire to live nor to reign longer than my life and reign shall be for your good. And though you have had and may have many mightier and wiser Princes sitting in this Seat, yet you never had nor shall have any that will love you better.

Thus Mr Speaker, I commend me to your loyal Loves, and yours to my best care and your further Councils, and I pray you Mr Comptrollor, and Mr Secretary, and you of my council, that before these Gentlemen depart into their Countries you bring them all to kiss my Hand.

Finis

"EULOGY FOR MAHATMA GANDHI"
Jawaharlal Nehru

On January 30, 1948, a disaffected Hindu assassinated Mohandas Ghandi. Jawaharlal Nehru – the first prime minister of independent India – made two moving speeches about the death and legacy of his friend. The first was a radio address on the same day; the second was the eulogy at his funeral on February 2.

He has gone, and all over India there is a feeling of having been left desolate and forlorn. All of us sense that feeling, and I do not know when we shall be able to get rid of it. And yet together with that feeling there is also a feeling of proud thankfulness that it has been given to us of this generation to be associated with this mighty person. In ages to come, centuries and maybe millennia after us, people will think of this generation when this man of God trod on earth, and will think of us who, however small, could also follow his path and tread the holy ground where his feet had been.

Let us be worthy of him.

RELIGION

"THE TEN COMMANDMENTS"
Moses

During the Israelites' 40 years in the wilderness, Moses spoke to God at the peak of Mount Sinai and received from him two stone tablets containing the Ten Commandments, and instructions for building a container to house them – the Ark of the Covenant. This text is taken from the King James version of the Bible, but put into the familiar order.

And God spake all these words, saying,
I am the LORD thy God, which have brought thee out of the land of Egypt, out of the house of bondage.
1. Thou shalt have no other gods before me.
2. Thou shalt not make unto thee any graven image, or any likeness of any thing that is in heaven above, or that is in the earth beneath, or that is in the water under the earth:
Thou shalt not bow down thyself to them, nor serve them: for I the LORD thy God am a jealous God, visiting the iniquity of the fathers upon the children unto the third and fourth generation of them that hate me;
And shewing mercy unto thousands of them that love me, and keep my commandments.

3. Thou shalt not take the name of the LORD thy God in vain; for the LORD will not hold him guiltless that taketh his name in vain.
4. Remember the sabbath day, to keep it holy.
Six days shalt thou labour, and do all thy work:
But the seventh day is the sabbath of the LORD thy God: in it thou shalt not do any work, thou, nor thy son, nor thy daughter, thy manservant, nor thy maidservant, nor thy cattle, nor thy stranger that is within thy gates:
For in six days the LORD made heaven and earth, the sea, and all that in them is, and rested the seventh day: wherefore the LORD blessed the sabbath day, and hallowed it.
5. Honour thy father and thy mother: that thy days may be long upon the land which the LORD thy God giveth thee.
6. Thou shalt not kill.
7. Thou shalt not commit adultery.
8. Thou shalt not steal.
9. Thou shalt not bear false witness against thy neighbour.
10. Thou shalt not covet thy neighbour's house, thou shalt not covet thy neighbour's wife, nor his manservant, nor his maidservant, nor his ox, nor his ass, nor any thing that is thy neighbour's.

"HERE I STAND"
Martin Luther

Four years after publishing his "95 theses", Martin Luther faced trial for heresy in 1520 in front of Emperor Charles V. The following is the speech he made in his defence.

Most serene emperor, and you illustrious princes and gracious lords, I this day appear before you in all humility, according to your command, and I implore your majesty and your august highnesses, by the mercies of God, to listen with favour to the defence of a cause which I am well assured is just and right. I ask pardon, if by reason of my ignorance, I am wanting in the manners that befit a court; for I have not been brought up in king's palaces, but in the seclusion of a cloister.

Two questions were yesterday put to me by his imperial majesty; the first, whether I was the author of the books whose titles were read; the second, whether I wished to revoke or defend the doctrine I have taught. I answered the first, and I adhere to that answer.

As to the second, I have composed writings on very different subjects. In some I have discussed Faith and Good Works, in a spirit at once so pure, clear, and Christian, that even my adversaries themselves, far from finding anything to censure, confess that these writings are profitable, and deserve to be perused by devout persons. The pope's bull, violent as it is, acknowledges this. What, then, should I be doing if I were now to retract these writings? Wretched man! I alone, of all men living, should be abandoning truths approved by the unanimous voice of friends and enemies, and opposing doctrines that the whole world glories in confessing!

I have composed, secondly, certain works against popery, wherein I have attacked such as by false doctrines, irregular lives, and scandalous examples, afflict the Christian world, and ruin the bodies and souls of men. And is not this confirmed by the grief of all who fear God? Is it not manifest that the laws and human doctrines of the popes entangle, vex, and distress the consciences of the faithful, while the crying and endless extortions of Rome engulf the property and wealth of Christendom, and more particularly of this illustrious nation?

If I were to revoke what I have written on that subject, what should I do...but strengthen this tyranny, and open a wider door to so many and flagrant impieties? Bearing down all resistance with fresh fury, we should behold these proud men swell, foam, and rage more than ever! And not merely would the yoke which now weighs down Christians be made more grinding by my retractation – it would thereby become, so to speak, lawful – for, by my retractation, it would receive confirmation from your most serene majesty, and all the States of the Empire. Great God! I should thus be like to an infamous cloak, used to hide and cover over every kind of malice and tyranny.

In the third and last place, I have written some books against private individuals, who had undertaken to defend the tyranny of Rome by destroying the faith. I freely confess that I may have attacked such persons with more violence than was consistent with my profession as an ecclesiastic: I do not think of myself as a saint; but neither can I retract these books, because I should, by so doing, sanction the impieties of my opponents, and they would thence take occasion to crush God's people with still more cruelty.

Yet, as I am a mere man, and not God, I will defend myself after the example of Jesus Christ, who said: "If I have spoken evil, bear witness against me." How much more should I, who am but dust and ashes, and so prone to error, desire that everyone should bring forward what he can against my doctrine.

Therefore, most serene emperor, and you illustrious princes, and all, whether high or low, who hear me, I implore you by the mercies of God to prove to me by the writings of the prophets and apostles that I am in error. As soon as I shall be convinced, I will instantly retract all my errors, and will myself be the first to seize my writings, and commit them to the flames.

What I have just said I think will clearly show that I have well considered and weighed the dangers to which I am exposing myself; but far from being dismayed by them, I rejoice exceedingly to see the Gospel this day, as of old, a cause of disturbance and disagreement. It is the character and destiny of God's word. "I came not to send peace unto the earth, but a sword," said Jesus Christ. God is wonderful and awful in His counsels. Let us have a care, lest in our endeavours to arrest discords, we be bound to fight against the holy word of God and bring down upon our heads a frightful deluge of inextricable dangers, present disaster, and everlasting desolations...Let us have a care lest the reign of the young and noble prince, the Emperor Charles, on whom, next to God, we build so many hopes, should not only commence, but continue and terminate its course under the most fatal auspices. I might cite examples drawn from the oracles of God. I might speak of Pharaohs, of kings of Babylon, or of Israel, who were never more contributing to their own ruin than when, by measures in appearances most prudent, they thought to establish their authority! "God removeth the mountains and they know not."

In speaking thus, I do not suppose that such noble princes have need of my poor judgment; but I wish to acquit myself of a duty that Germany has a right to expect from her children. And so commending myself to your august majesty, and your most serene highnesses, I beseech you, in all humility, not to permit the hatred of my enemies to rain upon me an indignation I have not deserved. Since your most serene majesty and your high mightinesses require of me a simple, clear and direct answer, I will give one, and it is this: I can not submit my faith either to the pope or to the council, because it is as clear as noonday that they have fallen into error and even into glaring inconsistency with themselves. If, then, I am not convinced by proof from Holy Scripture, or by cogent reasons, if I am not satisfied by the very text I have cited, and if my judgment is not in this way brought into subjection to God's word, I neither can nor will retract anything; for it cannot be right for a Christian to speak against his country. I stand here and can say no more. God help me. Amen.

"THE SERMON ON THE MOUNT"
Jesus Christ

This passage, from the Gospel according to St Matthew (Chapters 5–7), contains many of the basics tenets of the Christian faith, including the Lord's Prayer.

And seeing the multitudes, he went up into a mountain, and when he was seated, his disciples came unto him:

Then He opened His mouth and taught them, saying,

Blessed are the poor in spirit: for theirs is the kingdom of heaven.

Blessed are those that mourn: for they shall be comforted.

Blessed are the meek: for they shall inherit the earth.

Blessed are they which do hunger and thirst for righteousness: for they shall be filled.

Blessed are the merciful: for they shall obtain mercy.

Blessed are the pure in heart: for they shall see God.

Blessed are the peacemakers: for they shall be called the children of God.

Blessed are they which are persecuted for righteousness' sake: for theirs is the kingdom of heaven.

Blessed are ye when men shall revile you, and persecute you, and shall say all manner of evil against you falsely, for my sake. Rejoice and be exceeding glad: for great is your reward in heaven: for so persecuted were the prophets which were before you.

Ye are the salt of the earth: but if the salt have lost its flavour, wherewith shall it be salted? It is thenceforth good for nothing but to be cast out and trodden under the foot of men.

Ye are the light of the world. A city that is set on a hill cannot be hid.

Neither do men light a candle and put it under a bushel, but on a candlestick; and it giveth light unto all that are in the house.

Let your light so shine before men, that they may see your good works, and glorify your Father which is in heaven.

Think not that I am come to destroy the law, or the prophets: I am not come to destroy but to fulfil.

For verily, I say unto you. Till heaven and earth pass, one jot or one tittle shall in no wise pass from the law, till all be fulfilled.

Whosoever therefore shall break one of the least of these commandments, and shall teach men so, he shall be called least in the kingdom of heaven: but whosoever shall do and teach them, the same shall be called great in the kingdom of heaven.

For I say to you, That except your righteousness shall exceed the righteousness of the scribes and Pharisees, ye shall in no case enter the kingdom of heaven.

Ye have heard that it was said by them of old time, Thou shall not kill; and whosoever shall kill shall be in danger of the judgment:

But I say unto you, That whoever is angry with his brother without a cause shall be in danger of the judgment: and whoever shall say to his brother, Ra-ca, shall be in danger of the council: but whosoever shall say, Thou fool, shall be in danger of hell fire.

Therefore if thou bring thy gift before the altar, and there rememberest that thy brother hath ought against thee:

Leave there thy gift there before the altar, and go thy way; first be reconciled to thy brother, and then come and offer thy gift.

Agree with thine adversary quickly, whiles thou art in the way with him, lest at any time the adversary deliver thee to the judge, and the judge deliver thee to the officer, and thou be thrown into prison.

Verily, I say unto thee, Thou will by no means come out thence until you hast paid the uttermost farthing.

Ye have heard that it was said by them of old time, Thou shall not commit adultery:

But I say unto you, That whosoever looketh on a woman to lust for her hath committed adultery with her already in his heart.

And if thy right eye offend thee, pluck it out and cast it from thee:

for it is more profitable for thee that one of thy members should perish, and not that thy whole body should be cast into hell.

And if thy right hand offend thee, cut it off and cast it from thee for it is more profitable for thee that one of thy members should perish, and not that thy whole body should be cast into hell.

It hath been said, Whosoever shall put away his wife, let him give her a writing of divorcement.

But I say to you, That whosoever shall put away his wife, saving for the cause of fornication, causeth her to commit adultery: and whosoever marries a woman that is divorced committeth adultery.

Again, ye have heard that it was said by them of old time, Thou shalt not forswear thyself, but shalt perform unto the Lord thine oaths. But I say unto you, Swear not at all; neither by heaven; for it is God's throne:

Nor by the earth; for it is his footstool: neither by Jerusalem; for it is the city of the great King.

Neither shalt thou swear by thy head, because thou canst not make one hair white or black.

But let your communication be Yea, yea; Nay, nay: for whatsoever is more than these cometh of evil.

Ye have heard that it hath been said, An eye for an eye and a tooth for a tooth:

But I say unto you, That you resist not evil: but whosoever shall smite thee on thy right cheek, turn to him the other also.

If any man will sue thee at the law, and take away thy coat, let him have thy cloak also.

And whosoever shall compel thee to go a mile, go with him twain.

Give to him that asketh thee, and from him that would borrow from thee turn not thou away.

Ye have heard that it hath been said, Thou shalt love thy neighbour, and hate thine enemy.

But I say unto you, Love your enemies, bless them that curse you, do good to them that hate you, and pray for them which despitefully use you, and persecute you,

That ye may be the children of your Father which is in heaven: for he maketh his sun to rise on the evil and on the good, and sendeth rain on the just and on the unjust.

For if ye love them which love you, what reward have ye? Do not even the publicans the same?

And if ye salute your brethren only, what do ye more than others? Do not even the publicans so?

Be ye therefore perfect, even as your Father which is in heaven is perfect.

Take heed that ye do not your alms before men, to be seen of them: otherwise ye have no reward of your Father which is in heaven.

Therefore when thou doest thine alms, do not sound a trumpet before thee, as the hypocrites do in the synagogues and in the streets, that they may have glory of men. Verily I say unto you, They have their reward.

But when thou doest alms, let not thy left hand know what thy right hand doeth:

That thine alms may be in secret: and thy Father which seeth in secret himself shall reward thee openly.

And when thou prayest, thou shalt not be as the hypocrites are: for they love to pray standing in the synagogues and in the corners of the streets, that they may be seen of men. Verily I say unto you, They have their reward.

But thou, when thou prayest, enter into thy closet, and when thou hast shut thy door, pray to thy Father which is in secret; and thy Father which seeth in secret shall reward thee openly.

But when ye pray, use not vain repetitions, as the heathen do: for they think that they shall be heard for their much speaking.

Be not ye therefore like unto them: for your Father knoweth what things ye have need of, before ye ask him.

After this manner therefore pray ye: Our Father which art in heaven, Hallowed be thy name.

Thy kingdom come. Thy will be done in earth, as it is in heaven.

Give us this day our daily bread.

And forgive us our debts, as we forgive our debtors.

And lead us not into temptation, but deliver us from evil: for this is the kingdom, and the power, and the glory, for ever. Amen.

For if ye forgive men their trespasses, your heavenly Father will also forgive you:

But if ye forgive not men their trespasses, neither will your Father forgive your trespasses.

Moreover when ye fast, be not, as the hypocrites, of a sad countenance: for they disfigure their faces, that they may appear unto men to fast. Verily I say unto you, They have their reward.

But thou, when thou fastest, anoint thine head, and wash thy face:

That thou appear not unto men to fast, but unto thy Father which is in secret: and thy Father, which seeth in secret, shall reward thee openly.

Lay not up for yourselves treasures upon earth, where moth and rust doth corrupt, and where thieves break through and steal:

But lay up for yourselves treasures in heaven, where neither moth nor rust doth corrupt, and where thieves do not break through nor steal.

For where your treasure is, there will your heart be also.

The light of the body is the eye: if therefore thine eye be single, thy whole body shall be full of light.

But if thine eye be evil, thy whole body shall be full of darkness. If therefore the light that is in thee be darkness, how great is that darkness!

No man can serve two masters: for either he will hate the one, and love the other; or else he will hold to the one, and despise the other. Ye cannot serve God and mammon.

Therefore I say unto you; Take no thought for your life, what ye shall eat, or what ye shall drink; nor yet for your body, what ye shall put on. Is not the life more than meat, and the body more than raiment?

Behold the fowls of the air: for they sow not, neither do they reap, nor gather into barns; yet your heavenly Father feedeth them. Are ye not much better than they?

Which of you by taking thought can add one cubit unto his stature?

And why take ye thought for raiment? Consider the lilies of the field, how they grow; they toil not, neither do they spin:

And yet I say unto you, That even Solomon in all his glory was not arrayed like one of these.

Wherefore, if God so clothe the grass of the field, which to day is, and to morrow is cast into the oven, shall he not much more clothe you, O ye of little faith?

Therefore take no thought, saying, What shall we eat? Or, What shall we drink? Or, Wherewithal shall we be clothed?

For after all these things do the Gentiles seek? For your heavenly Father knoweth that ye have need of all these things.

But seek ye first the kingdom of God, and his righteousness; and all these things shall be added unto you.

Take therefore no thought for the morrow: for the morrow shall take thought for the things of itself. Sufficient unto the day is the evil thereof.

Judge not, that ye be not judged.

For with what judgment ye judge, ye shall be judged; and with what measure ye mete, it shall be measured to you again.

And why beholdest thou the mote that is in thy brother's eye, but considerest not the beam that is in thine own eye?

Or how wilt though say to thy brother, Let me pull out the mote out of thine eye; and, behold a beam is in thine own eye.

Thou hypocrite, first cast out the beam out of thine own eye; and then shalt thou see clearly to cast out the mote out of thy brother's eye.

Give not that which is holy unto the dogs, neither cast ye your pearls before swine, lest they trample them under their feet, and turn again and rend you.

Ask, and it shall be given you; seek, and ye shall find; knock, and it shall be opened unto you:

For every one that asketh receiveth; and he that seeketh findeth; and to him that knocketh it shall be opened.

Or what man is there of you, whom if his son ask bread, will he give him a stone?

Or if he ask a fish, will he give him a serpent?

If ye then, being evil, know how to give good gifts unto your children, how much more shall your Father which is in heaven give good things to them that ask him?

Therefore all things whatsoever ye would that men should do to you, do ye even so to them: for this is the law and the prophets.

Enter ye in at the strait gate: for wide is the gate, and broad is the way, that leadeth to destruction, and many there be which go in thereat:

Beware of false prophets, which come to you in sheep's clothing, but inwardly they are ravening wolves.

Ye shall know them by their fruits. Do men gather grapes of thorns, or figs of thistles?

Even so every good tree bringeth forth good fruit; but a corrupt tree bringeth forth evil fruit.

A good tree cannot bring forth evil fruit, neither can a corrupt tree bring forth good fruit.

Every tree that bringeth not forth good fruit is hewn down, and cast into the fire.

Wherefore by their fruits ye shall know them.

Not every one that saith unto me, Lord, Lord, shall enter into the kingdom of heaven; but he that doeth the will of my Father which is in heaven.

Many will say to me in that day, Lord, Lord, have we not prophesied in they name? And in thy name have cast out devils? And in thy name done many wonderful works?

And then will I profess unto them, I never knew you: depart from me, ye that work iniquity.

Therefore whosoever heareth these sayings of mine, and doeth them, I will liken him unto a wise man, which built his house upon a rock:

And the rain descended, and the floods came, and the winds blew, and beat upon that house; and it fell not: for it was founded upon a rock.

And every one that heareth these sayings of mine, and doeth them not, shall be likened unto a foolish man, which built his house upon the sand:

And the rain descended, and the floods came, and the winds blew, and beat upon that house; and it fell: and great was the fall of it.

"TURN THY FACE TOWARDS THE SACRED MOSQUE"

Allah, as taught to Muhammad

In 610, Gabriel appeared to Muhammad on Mount Hira near Mecca and made the first of a series of revelations of the word of Allah to him and taught him to recite it. The angel made further revelations to the prophet during the ensuing 22 years. The following passage forms part of the basic tenets of Moslem worship.

...We see thee often turn about thy face in the heavens, but we will surely turn thee to a qibla [the direction of Mecca] thou shalt like. Turn then thy face towards the Sacred Mosque; wherever ye be, turn your faces towards it; for verily, those who have the Book know that it is the truth from their Lord;– God is not careless of that which ye do.

And if thou shouldst bring to those who have been given the Book every sign, they would not follow your qibla; and thou art not to follow their qibla; nor do some of them follow the qibla of the others: and if thou followest their lusts after the knowledge that has come to thee then art thou of the evildoers.

Those whom we have given the Book know him as they know their sons, although a sect of them do surely hide the truth, the while they know.

The truth (is) from thy Lord; be not therefore one of those who doubt thereof.

Every sect has some one side to which they turn (in prayer); but do ye hasten onwards to good works; wherever ye are God will bring you all together; verily, God is mighty over all.

From whencesoever thou comest forth, there turn thy face towards the Sacred Mosque, for it is surely truth from thy Lord; God is not careless about what ye do.

And from whencesoever thou comest forth, there turn thy face towards the Sacred Mosque, and wheresoever ye are, turn your faces towards it, that men may have no argument against you, save only those of them who are unjust; and fear them not, but fear me and I will fulfil my favours to you, perchance ye may be guided yet.

Thus have we sent amongst you an apostle of yourselves, to recite to you our signs, to purify you and teach you the Book and wisdom, and to teach you what ye did not know; remember me, then, and I will remember you; thank me, and do not misbelieve.

O ye who do believe, seek aid from patience and from prayer, verily, God is with the patient.

"FIRE SERMON"
Siddhartha Gautama

Siddhartha Gautama – the Buddha – delivered this discourse more than 2,500 years ago. It is one of the fundamental scriptures of Buddhism and explains the concept of Enlightenment.

All things, O priests, are on fire. And what, O priests, are all these things which are on fire?

The eye, O priests, is on fire; forms are on fire; eye-consciousness is on fire; impressions received by the eye are on fire; and whatever sensation, pleasant, unpleasant, or indifferent, originates in dependence on impressions received by the eye, that is also on fire.

And with what are these on fire?

With the fire of passion, say I, with the fire of hatred, with the fire of infatuation; with birth, old age, death, sorrow, lamentation, misery, grief and despair are they on fire.

The ear is on fire; sounds are on fire;...the nose is on fire; odours are on fire;...the tongue is on fire; tastes are on fire;...the body is on fire; things tangible are on fire;...the mind is on fire; ideas are on fire;...mind-consciousness is on fire; impressions received by the mind are on fire; and whatever sensation, pleasant, unpleasant or indifferent, originates in dependence on impressions received by the mind, that is also on fire.

And with what are these on fire?

With the fire of passion, say I, with the fire of hatred, with the fire of infatuation; with birth, old age, death, sorrow, lamentation, misery, grief and despair are they on fire.

Perceiving this, O priests, the learned and noble disciple conceives an aversion for the eye, conceives an aversion for forms, conceives an aversion for eye-consciousness, conceives an aversion for the impressions received by the eye; and whatever sensation, pleasant, unpleasant, or indifferent, originates in dependence on impressions received by the eye, for that also he conceives an aversion. Conceives an aversion for the ear, conceives an aversion for sounds,...conceives an aversion for the nose, conceives an aversion for odours,...conceives an aversion for the tongue, conceives an aversion for the mind, conceives an aversion for ideas, conceives an aversion for the body, conceives an aversion for things tangible,...conceives an aversion for the mind, conceives an aversion for ideas, conceives an aversion for mind-consciousness, conceives an aversion for the impressions received by the mind; and whatever sensation, pleasant, unpleasant, or indifferent, originates in dependence on impressions received by the mind, for this also he conceives an aversion. And in conceiving this aversion, he becomes divested of passion, and by the absence of passion he becomes free, and when he is free he becomes aware that he is free; and he knows that rebirth is exhausted, that he has lived the holy life, that he has done what it behooved him to do, and that he is no more for this world...

"ON PERSECUTION"
John Calvin

The influence of this 16th-century French Protestant reformer was second only to that of Martin Luther himself. A strict moralist, he firmly believed that in order to gain God's grace one had to undergo suffering, persecution and trials while alive.

The apostle says, "Let us go forth from the city after the Lord Jesus, bearing his reproach." In the first place he reminds us, although the swords should not be drawn over us nor the fired kindles to burn us, that we cannot be truly united to the Son of God while we are rooted in this world. Wherefore, a Christian, even in repose, must always have one foot lifted to march to battle, and not only so, but he must have his affections withdrawn from the world although his body is dwelling in it. Grant that this at first sight seems to us hard; still, we must be satisfied with the words of Saint Paul, "We are called and appointed to suffer." As if he had said, Such is our condition as Christians; this is the road by which we must go if we would follow Christ.

Meanwhile, to solace our infirmity and mitigate the vexation and sorrow which persecution might cause us, a good reward is held forth: in suffering for the cause of God, we are walking step by step after the Son of God and have him for our guide. Were it simply said that to be Christians we must pass through all the insults of the world boldly, to meet death at all times and in whatever way God may be pleased to appoint, we might apparently have some pretext for replying. It is a stange road to go at a peradventure. But when we are commanded to follow the Lord Jesus, his guidance is too good and honourable to be refused.

Are we so delicate as to be unwilling to endure anything? Then we must renounce the grace of God by which he has called us to the hope of salvation. For there are two things which cannot be separated – to be members of Christ, and to be tried by many afflictions. We certainly ought to prize such a conformity to the Son of God much more than we do. It is true that in the world's judgment there is disgrace in suffering for the Gospel. But since we know that unbelievers are blind, ought we not to have better eyes than they? It is ignominy to suffer from those who occupy the seat of justice, but Saint Paul shows us by his example that we have to glory in scourgings for Jesus Christ, as marks by which God recognizes us and avows us for his own. And we know what Saint Luke narrates of Peter and John; namely, that they rejoiced to have been "counted worthy to suffer infamy and reproach for the name of the Lord Jesus".

Ignominy and dignity are two opposites: so says the world, which, being infatuated, judges against all reason, and in this way converts the glory of god into dishonour. But, on our part, let us not refuse to be vilified as concerns the world, in order to be honoured before God and his angels. We see what pains the ambitious take to receive the commands of a king, and what a boast they make of it. The Son of God presents his commands to us, and everyone stands back! Tell me, pray, whether in so doing are we worthy of having anything in common with him? There is nothing here to attract our sensual nature, but such, notwithstanding, are the true escutcheons of nobility in the heavens. Imprisonment, exile, evil report, imply in men's imagination whatever is to be vituperated; but what hinders us from viewing things as God judges and declares them, save our unbelief? Wherefore let the name of the Son of God have all the weight with us which it deserves, that we may learn to count it honour when he stamps his marks upon us. If we act otherwise, our ingratitude is insupportable.

Were God to deal with us according to our deserts, would he not have just cause to chastise us daily in a thousand ways? Nay, more, a hundred thousand deaths would not suffice for a small portion of our misdeeds! Now, if in his infinite goodness he puts all our faults under his foot and abolishes them and, instead of punishing us according to our demerit, devises an admirable means to convert our afflictions into honour and a special privilege, inasmuch as through them we are taken into partnership with his Son, must it not be said, when we disdain such a happy state, that we have indeed made little progress in Christian doctrine?

It were easy indeed for God to crown us at once without requiring us to sustain any combats; but as it is his pleasure that until the end of the world Christ shall reign in the midst of his enemies, so it is also his pleasure that we, being placed in the midst of them, shall suffer their oppression and violence till he deliver us. I know, indeed, that the flesh kicks when it is to be brought to this point, but still the will of God must have the mastery. If we feel some repugnance in ourselves it need not surprise us; for it is only too natural for us to shun the cross. Still, let us not fail to surmount it, knowing that God accepts our obedience, provided we bring all our feelings and wishes into captivity and make them subject to him.

In ancient times vast numbers of people, to obtain a simple crown of leaves, refused no toil, no pain, no trouble; nay, it even cost them nothing to die, and yet every one of them fought for a peradventure, not knowing whether he was to gain or lose the prize. God holds forth to us the immortal crown by which we may become partakers of his glory. He does not mean us to fight a haphazard, but all of us have a promise of the prize for which we strive. Have we any cause, then, to decline the struggle? Do we think it has been said in vain, "If we die with Jesus Christ we shall also live with him"? Our triumph is prepared, and yet we do all we can to shun the combat.

"THE OPIUM OF THE PEOPLE"
Karl Marx

The 19th-century German philosopher and revolutionary believed that religion was used by those in power as a tool to keep the people under control. The last sentence is often misquoted as "the opiate of the masses". Marx's ideas had a profound effect on the method of government in Russia after the revolution of 1917 and so over the whole of the Soviet bloc during the 20th century.

Religion is the sigh of the oppressed creature, the heart of a heartless world, and the soul of soulless conditions. It is the opium of the people.

SCIENCE

"WE CHOOSE TO GO TO THE MOON"
John F. Kennedy

Exactly 17 months after the Soviet cosmonaut Yuri Gagarin became the first human to go into space on April 12, 1961, President John F. Kennedy – at Rice University Stadium, Houston, Texas – announced an ambitious programme to allow an American to walk on the surface of the moon before the end of the 1960s.

President Pitzer, Mr Vice President, Governor, Congressman Thomas, Senator Wiley and Congressman Miller, Mr Webb, Mr Bell, scientists, distinguished guests, and ladies and gentlemen:

I appreciate your president having made me an honorary visiting professor, and I will assure you that my first lecture will be very brief.

I am delighted to be here and I'm particularly delighted to be here on this occasion.

We meet at a college noted for knowledge, in a city noted for progress, in a State noted for strength, and we stand in need of all three, for we meet in an hour of change and challenge, in a decade of hope and fear, in an age of both knowledge and ignorance. The greater our knowledge increases, the greater our ignorance unfolds.

Despite the striking fact that most of the scientists that the world has ever known are alive and working today, despite the fact that this Nation's own scientific manpower is doubling every 12 years in a rate of growth more than three times that of our population as a whole, despite that, the vast stretches of the unknown and the unanswered and the unfinished still far outstrip our collective comprehension.

No man can fully grasp how far and how fast we have come, but condense, if you will, the 50,000 years of man's recorded history in a time span of but a half-century. Stated in these terms, we know very little about the first 40 years, except at the end of them advanced man had learned to use the skins of animals to cover them. Then about 10 years ago, under this standard, man emerged from his caves to construct other kinds of shelter. Only five years ago man learned to write and use a cart with wheels. Christianity began less than two years ago. The printing press came this year, and then less than two months ago, during this whole 50-year span of human history, the steam engine provided a new source of power.

Newton explored the meaning of gravity. Last month electric lights and telephones and automobiles and airplanes became available. Only last week did we develop penicillin and television and nuclear power, and now if America's new spacecraft succeeds in reaching Venus, we will have literally reached the stars before midnight tonight.

This is a breathtaking pace, and such a pace cannot help but create new ills as it dispels old, new ignorance, new problems, new dangers. Surely the opening vistas of space promise high costs and hardships, as well as high reward.

So it is not surprising that some would have us stay where we are a little longer to rest, to wait. But this city of Houston, this State of

Texas, this country of the United States was not built by those who waited and rested and wished to look behind them. This country was conquered by those who moved forward – and so will space.

William Bradford, speaking in 1630 of the founding of the Plymouth Bay Colony, said that all great and honourable actions are accompanied with great difficulties, and both must be enterprised and overcome with answerable courage.

If this capsule history of our progress teaches us anything, it is that man, in his quest for knowledge and progress, is determined and cannot be deterred. The exploration of space will go ahead, whether we join in it or not, and it is one of the great adventures of all time, and no nation which expects to be the leader of other nations can expect to stay behind in the race for space.

Those who came before us made certain that this country rode the first waves of the industrial revolutions, the first waves of modern invention, and the first wave of nuclear power, and this generation does not intend to founder in the backwash of the coming age of space. We mean to be a part of it – we mean to lead it. For the eyes of the world now look into space, to the moon and to the planets beyond, and we have vowed that we shall not see it governed by a hostile flag of conquest, but by a banner of freedom and peace. We have vowed that we shall not see space filled with weapons of mass destruction, but with instruments of knowledge and understanding.

Yet the vows of this Nation can only be fulfilled if we in this Nation are first, and, therefore, we intend to be first. In short, our leadership in science and in industry, our hopes for peace and security, our obligations to ourselves as well as others, all require us to make this effort, to solve these mysteries, to solve them for the good of all men, and to become the world's leading space-faring nation.

We set sail on this new sea because there is new knowledge to be gained, and new rights to be won, and they must be won and used for the progress of all people. For space science, like nuclear science and all technology, has no conscience of its own. Whether it will become a force for good or ill depends on man, and only if the United States occupies a position of pre-eminence can we help decide whether this new ocean will be a sea of peace or a new terrifying theatre of war. I do not say that we should or will go unprotected against the hostile misuse of space any more than we go unprotected against the hostile use of land or sea, but I do say that space can be explored and mastered without feeding the fires of war, without repeating the mistakes that man has made in extending his writ around this globe of ours.

There is no strife, no prejudice, no national conflict in outer space as yet. Its hazards are hostile to us all. Its conquest deserves the best of all mankind, and its opportunity for peaceful cooperation may never come again. But why, some say, the moon? Why choose this as our goal? And they may well ask why climb the highest mountain? Why, 35 years ago, fly the Atlantic? Why does Rice play Texas?

We choose to go to the moon. We choose to go to the moon in this decade and do the other things, not because they are easy, but because they are hard, because that goal will serve to organize and measure the best of our energies and skills, because that challenge is one that we are willing to accept, one we are unwilling to postpone, and one which we intend to win, and the others, too.

It is for these reasons that I regard the decision last year to shift our efforts in space from low to high gear as among the most important decisions that will be made during my incumbency in the office of the Presidency.

In the last 24 hours we have seen facilities now being created for the greatest and most complex exploration in man's history. We have felt the ground shake and the air shattered by the testing of a Saturn C-1 booster rocket, many times as powerful as the Atlas which launched John Glenn, generating power equivalent to 10,000 automobiles with their accelerators on the floor. We have seen the site where the F-1 rocket engines, each one as powerful as all eight engines of the Saturn combined, will be clustered together to make the advanced Saturn missile, assembled in a new building to be built at Cape Canaveral as tall as a 48-storey structure, as wide as a city block, and as long as two lengths of this field.

Within these last 19 months at least 45 satellites have circled the earth. Some 40 of them were "made in the United States of America" and they were far more sophisticated and supplied far more knowledge to the people of the world than those of the Soviet Union.

The Mariner spacecraft now on its way to Venus is the most intricate instrument in the history of space science. The accuracy of that shot is comparable to firing a missile from Cape Canaveral and dropping it in this stadium between the the 40-yard lines.

Transit satellites are helping our ships at sea to steer a safer course. Tiros satellites have given us unprecedented warnings of hurricanes and storms, and will do the same for forest fires and icebergs.

We have had our failures, but so have others, even if they do not admit them. And they may be less public.

To be sure, we are behind, and will be behind for some time in manned flight. But we do not intend to stay behind, and in this decade, we shall make up and move ahead.

The growth of our science and education will be enriched by new knowledge of our universe and environment, by new techniques of learning and mapping and observation, by new tools and computers for industry, medicine, the home as well as the school. Technical institutions, such as Rice, will reap the harvest of these gains.

And finally, the space effort itself, while still in its infancy, has already created a great number of new companies, and tens of thousands of new jobs. Space and related industries are generating new demands in investment and skilled personnel, and this city and this State, and this region, will share greatly in this growth. What was once the furthest outpost on the old frontier of the West will be the furthest outpost on the new frontier of science and space. Houston, your City of Houston, with its Manned Spacecraft Center, will become the heart of a large scientific and engineering community. During the next five years the National Aeronautics and Space Administration expects to double the number of scientists and engineers in this area, to increase its outlays for salaries and expenses to $60 million a year; to invest some $200 million in plant and laboratory facilities; and to direct or contract for new space efforts over $1 billion from this Center in this City.

To be sure, all this costs us all a good deal of money. This year's space budget is three times what it was in January 1961, and it is greater than the space budget of the previous eight years combined. That budget now stands at $5,400 million a year – a staggering sum, though somewhat less than we pay for cigarettes and cigars every year. Space expenditures will soon rise some more, from 40 cents per person per week to more than 50 cents a week for every man, woman and child in the United States, for we have given this programme a high national priority – even though I realize that this is in some measure an act of faith and vision, for we do not now know what benefits await us.

But if I were to say, my fellow citizens, that we shall send to the moon, 240,000 miles away from the control station in Houston, a giant rocket more than 300 feet tall, the length of this football field, made of new metal alloys, some of which have not yet been invented, capable of standing heat and stresses several times more than have ever been experienced, fitted together with a precision better than the finest watch, carrying all the equipment needed for propulsion, guidance, control, communications, food and survival, on an untried mission, to an unknown celestial body, and then return it safely to earth, re-entering the atmosphere at speeds of over 25,000 miles per hour, causing heat about half that of the temperature of the sun – almost as hot as it is here today – and do all this, and do it right, and do it first before this decade is out – then we must be bold.

I'm the one who is doing all the work, so we just want you to stay cool for a minute.

However, I think we're going to do it, and I think that we must pay what needs to be paid. I don't think we ought to waste any money, but I think we ought to do the job. And this will be done in the decade of the sixties. It may be done while some of you are still here at school at this college and university. It will be done during the term of office of some of the people who sit here on this platform. But it will be done. And it will be done before the end of this decade.

I am delighted that this university is playing a part in putting a man on the moon as part of a great national effort of the United States of America.

Many years ago the great British explorer George Mallory, who was to die on Mount Everest, was asked why did he want to climb it. He said, "Because it is there."

Well, space is there, and we're going to climb it, and the moon and the planets are there, and new hopes for knowledge and peace are there. And, therefore, as we set sail we ask God's blessing on the most hazardous and dangerous and greatest adventure on which man has ever embarked.

Thank you.

“THE EAGLE HAS LANDED”
Neil Armstrong

On July 20, 1969, Apollo 11’s Lunar Module approached the moon’s surface with astronauts Neil Armstrong and Edwin “Buzz” Aldrin. Michael Collins stayed in orbit in the Command Module.

750 feet, coming down at 23 degrees...700 feet, 21 down...400 feet, down at nine...Got the shadow out there...75 feet, things looking good...lights on...picking up some dust... 0 feet, 2½ down...faint shadow...four forward...drifting to the right a little...contact light...O.K. Engine stop...Houston. Tranquility Base here. The Eagle has landed.”

“...ONE SMALL STEP”
Neil Armstrong

Some 4½ hours after landing, Neil Armstrong emerged from the hatchway and descended the Lunar Module’s steps, as the first person ever to walk on another astronomical body.

That’s one small step for man, one giant leap for mankind.

"EPPUR, SI MUOVE"
Galileo Galilei

In the 17th century to disagree with the Ptolemaic, earth-centred model of the solar system accepted as part of Church doctrine was seen by many to be an attack on the Church itself. In 1633 Galileo Galilei was put on trial for heresy for his book, *Dialogue concerning the Two Chief World Systems*. He was forced to recant, and on June 22 made the abjuration below.

Desiring to remove from the minds of your Eminences, and of all faithful Christians, this strong suspicion, reasonably conceived against me, with sincere heart and unfeigned faith I abjure, curse, and detest the aforesaid errors and heresies, and generally every other error and sect whatsoever contrary to the said Holy Church; and I swear that in the future I will never again say or assert, verbally or in writing, anything that might furnish occasion for a similar suspicion regarding me...

I, the said Galileo Galilei, have abjured, sworn, promised, and bound myself as above; and in witness of the truth thereof I have with my own hand subscribed the present document of my abjuration, and recited it word for word at Rome, in the Convent of Minerva, this twenty-second day of June, 1633.

I, Galileo Galilei, have abjured as above with my own hand.

As legend has it, as he got off his knees he is said to have muttered under his breath, "*Eppur, si muove*" ("Yet, it moves"), referring to the earth.

"HOUSTON, WE'VE HAD A PROBLEM"
Jack Swigert Jr, Jim Lovell, Fred Haise

On April 11, 1970, Apollo 13, the third NASA mission to the moon, took off normally. However, just over two days into the mission, one of the three oxygen tanks on the Service Module exploded, damaging a second and taking out the Command Module's power systems. The following four days were nerve-wracking as one mistake could have led to the deaths of the three astronauts. The incident helped to curtail the Apollo programme. Duke is Charlie Duke, who was relaying radio communications between Houston and Apollo 13.

55:55:20 – Swigert: "OK, Houston, we've had a problem here."

55:55:28 – Duke: "This is Houston. Say again please."

55:55:35 – Lovell: "Houston, we've had a problem. We've had a main B bus undervolt". [power loss]

55:55:42 – Duke: "Roger. Main B undervolt."

55:55:49 – Oxygen tank No. 2 temperature begins steady drop lasting 59 seconds indicating a failed sensor.

55:56:10 – Haise: "Okay. Right now, Houston, the voltage is – is looking good. And we had a pretty large bang associated with the caution and warning there. And as I recall, main B was the one that had an amp spike on it once before."

55:56:30 – Duke: "Roger, Fred."

55:56:38 – Oxygen tank No. 2 quantity becomes erratic for 69 seconds before assuming an off-scale low state, indicating a failed sensor.

55:56:54 – Haise: "In the interim here, we're starting to go ahead and button up the tunnel again."

55:57:04 – Haise: "That jolt must have rocked the sensor on – see now – oxygen quantity 2. It was oscillating down around 20 to 60 per cent. Now it's full-scale high."

55:57:39 – Master caution and warning triggered by DC main bus B undervoltage. Alarm is turned off in 6 seconds.

55:57:40 – DC main bus B drops below 26.25 volts and continues to fall rapidly.

55:57:44 – Lovell: "Okay. And we're looking at our service module RCS helium 1. We have – B is barber poled and D is barber poled, helium 2, D is barber pole, and secondary propellants, I have A and C barber pole." **AC bus fails within 2 seconds.**

55:57:45 – Fuel cell 3 fails.

55:57:59 – Fuel cell current begins to decrease.

55:58:02 – Master caution and warning caused by AC bus 2 being reset.

55:58:06 – Master caution and warning triggered by DC main bus undervoltage.

55:58:07 – DC main bus A drops below 26.25 volts and in the next few seconds levels off at 25.5 volts.

55:58:07 – Haise: "AC 2 is showing zip."

55:58:25 – Haise: "Yes, we got a main bus A undervolt now, too, showing. It's reading about 25 and a half. Main B is reading zip right now."

"DOLLY THE SHEEP"
Ian Wilmut

In December 1997, an article in *Science* magazine detailed the work of scientists at the Roslin Institute in Edinburgh that had resulted in the birth 17 months earlier of Dolly the sheep, the first to have been cloned from an adult cell rather than an embryonic stem cell. Reactions varied from those who thought that this would lead to advances in medicine to those who feared its implication for the possible cloning of humans.

Our ability now to modify and select cells in culture and then produce transgenic lambs by nuclear transfer is tremendously encouraging and a major step towards our goal of being able to make very precise genetic modifications in livestock species.

"MOLECULAR STRUCTURE OF NUCLEIC ACIDS"
James Watson and Francis Crick

In a paper in *Nature* magazine on April 2, 1953 Watson and Crick announced the results of their team's research into the structures that allow cells to reproduce. This discovery led the way for everything that has been discovered since about genes and inheritence.

We wish to put forward a radically different structure for the salt of deoxyribose nucleic acid. This structure has two helical chains each coiled round the same axis.

If it is assumed that the bases only occur in the structure in the most plausible tautomeric forms (that is, with the keto rather than the enol configurations) it is found that only specific pairs of bases can bond together. These pairs are: adenine (purine) with thymine (pyrimidine), and guanine (purine) with cytosine (pyrimidine).

...It has not escaped our notice that the specific pairing we have postulated immediately suggests a possible copying mechanism for the genetic material.

"HUMAN GENOME MAPPING PROJECT"
Michael Dexter

On June 26, 2000, an international team of geneticists announced the results of years of cooperation between institutions: the first draft map of the human genome – the complete sequence of DNA in a human cell. Dr Michael Dexter of the Wellcome Institute in Britain summed up the team's euphoria at completing research that could lead to the eradication of genetic disease.

This is the outstanding achievement not only of our lifetime, but in terms of human history. I say this, because the Human Genome Project does have the potential to impact on the life of every person on this planet.

PATRIOTISM

"THE ARMADA SPEECH"
Elizabeth I

In May 1588, Philip II of Spain sent a fleet of 131 ships with more than 17,000 troops to invade England. When they arrived at Calais to collect 16,000 more soldiers, invasion seemed imminent. On August 9, Elizabeth I addressed her forces at Tilbury docks. Sir Francis Drake's fireships scared the Armada's commanders into setting sail for the English Channel, where they were met by the faster and better armed English fleet. Escaping to the North Sea, the Spanish were then scattered by appalling weather. Only a third of the Spanish men lived to return home.

My loving people, we have been persuaded by some, that are careful of our safety, to take heed how we commit ourselves to armed multitudes, for fear of treachery; but I assure you, I do not desire to live to distrust my faithful and loving people.

Let tyrants fear; I have always so behaved myself that, under God,

I have placed my chiefest strength and safeguard in the loyal hearts and good will of my subjects. And therefore I am come amongst you at this time, not as for my recreation or sport, but being resolved, in the midst and heat of the battle, to live or die amongst you all; to lay down, for my God, and for my kingdom, and for my people, my honour and my blood, even in the dust.

I know I have but the body of a weak and feeble woman; but I have the heart of a king, and of a king of England, too; and think foul scorn that Parma or Spain, or any prince of Europe, should dare to invade the borders of my realms: to which, rather than any dishonour should grow by me, I myself will take up arms; I myself will be your general, judge, and rewarder of every one of your virtues in the field.

I know already, by your forwardness, that you have deserved rewards and crowns; and we do assure you, on the word of a prince, they shall be duly paid you. In the mean my lieutenant general shall be in my stead, than whom never prince commanded a more noble and worthy subject; not doubting by your obedience to my general, by your concord in the camp, and by your valour in the field, we shall shortly have a famous victory over the enemies of my God, of my kingdom, and of my people.

"FAREWELL TO THE OLD GUARD"
Napoleon Bonaparte

After more than 20 years ruling France, Napoleon was defeated by the allied army and forced to abdicate on April 6, 1814. Two weeks later, he addressed the remaining officers of his "old guard", before being exiled to the Mediterranean island of Elba. He escaped ten months later and briefly regained control of his army before his final defeat on June 18, 1815. He died six years later in exile on the island of St Helena in the south Atlantic.

Soldiers of my Old Guard: I bid you farewell. For 20 years I have constantly accompanied you on the road to honour and glory. In these latter times, as in the days of our prosperity, you have invariably been models of courage and fidelity. With men such as you our cause could not be lost; but the war would have been interminable; it would have been civil war, and that would have entailed deeper misfortunes on France.

I have sacrificed all of my interests to those of the country. I go, but you, my friends, will continue to serve France. Her happiness was my only thought. It will still be the object of my wishes. Do not regret my fate; if I have consented to survive, it is to serve your glory. I intend to write the history of the great achievements we have performed together. Adieu, my friends. Would I could press you all to my heart.

"THE GETTYSBURG ADDRESS"
Abraham Lincoln

On November 19, 1863, Lincoln rededicated the cemetary at Gettysburg to the ideals with which America had been founded. Earlier in the year more than 51,000 troops had been killed, wounded or gone missing during the biggest battle of the American Civil War.

Fourscore and seven years ago our fathers brought forth on this continent a new nation, conceived in liberty and dedicated to the proposition that all men are created equal.

Now we are engaged in a great civil war, testing whether that nation or any nation so conceived and so dedicated can long endure. We are met on a great battlefield of that war. We have come to dedicate a portion of it as a final resting place for those who died here that the nation might live. This we may, in all propriety, do. But in a larger sense, we cannot dedicate, we cannot consecrate, we cannot hallow this ground. The brave men, living and dead, who struggled here have hallowed it far above our poor power to add or detract. The world will little note nor long remember what we say here, but it can never forget what they did here.

It is rather for us, the living, we here be dedicated to the great task remaining before us – that from these honoured dead we take increased devotion to that cause for which they here gave the last full measure of devotion – that we here highly resolve that these dead shall not have died in vain, that this nation shall have a new birth of freedom, and that government of the people, by the people, for the people shall not perish from the earth.

"...WE NEED TO DARE, TO DARE AGAIN, ALWAYS TO DARE!"
Georges Jacques Danton

This rousing speech was made on September 2, 1792, the same day that news reached Paris that Verdun was under siege by the invading Prussian army. The King and Queen of France had been taken prisoner just a month earlier and Danton's exhortation to put to death any people who did not mobilize is chilling in the light of the wholesale massacre that was already occurring in Paris.

It is satisfying for the ministers of the free people to be able to announce to them that their country will be saved. All are moved, all are stirred, all burn to enter the combat.

You know that Verdun is by no means yet in the power of our enemies and that its garrison swears to sacrifice the first who proposes surrender.

One portion of our people will be mobilized to the frontiers, another will dig the entrenchments and the third, armed with pikes, will defend the interior of our cities. Paris will support these great efforts. The commissioners of the Commune will solemnly proclaim to the citizens the invitation to arm and march to the defence of the country. It is now, gentlemen, that you can proclaim that the capital deserves [the support of] all of France. It is now that this National Assembly becomes a true committee of war. We ask that you work with us in directing this sublime movement of the people, by naming commissioners who will assist us in all these great measures. We ask for anyone refusing to serve in person or to take up arms again to be punished by death. We ask for instructions to be given to the people to direct their movements. We ask for couriers to be sent to all the departments [administrative regions] to notify them of the decrees that you proclaim here. The tocsin we shall sound is in no way an alarm signal; it orders the attack on the enemies of the country. To defeat them we need to dare, to dare again, always to dare, and France will be saved!

"JUSTICE FOR IRELAND"
Daniel O'Connell

Until 1800, the Irish had a separate parliament in Dublin, but in that year the British Act of Union abolished it and took control to London. One of the side-effects was that anti-Catholic legislation there meant that Ireland's 80-per-cent Catholic population could not be represented by Catholic MPs. In 1828, Daniel O'Connell ran for Parliament and won by a huge margin. He could not take his seat, but the British prime minister realized that reform was needed and in 1829 the Catholic Emancipation Act was passed, allowing Catholics to become MPs in London. O'Connell took his seat and became a forceful speaker for the Irish cause. This example dates from February 4, 1836, after the King's speech at the opening of Parliament.

It appears to me impossible to suppose that the House will consider me presumptuous in wishing to be heard for a short time on this question, especially after the distinct manner in which I have been alluded to in the course of the debate. If I had no other excuse, that would be sufficient; but I do not want it; I have another and a better – the question is one in the highest degree interesting to the people of Ireland. It is, whether we mean to do justice to that country – whether we mean to continue the injustice which has been already done to it, or to hold out the hope that it will be treated in the same manner as England and Scotland. That is the question. We know what "lip service" is; we do not want that. There are some men who will even declare that they are willing to refuse justice to Ireland; while there are others who, though they are ashamed to say so, are ready to consummate the iniquity, and they do so.

England never did do justice to Ireland – she never did. What we have got of it we have extorted from men opposed to us on principle – against which principle they have made us such concessions as we have obtained from them. The right honourable baronet opposite says he does not distinctly understand what is meant by a principle. I believe him. He advocated religious exclusion on religious motives; he yielded that point at length, when we were strong enough to make it prudent for him to do so.

Here am I calling for justice to Ireland; but there is a coalition tonight – not a base unprincipled one – God forbid! – it is an extremely natural one; I mean that between the right honourable baronet and the noble lord the member for North Lancashire. It is a natural coalition, and it is impromptu; for the noble lord informs us he had not even a notion of taking the part he has until the moment at which he seated himself where he now is. I know his candor; he told us it was a sudden inspiration which induced him to take part against Ireland. I believe it with the most potent faith, because I know that he requires no preparation for voting against the interests of the Irish people. [Groans from other members.] I thank you for that groan – it is just of a piece with the rest. I regret much that I have been thrown upon arguing this particular question, because I should have liked to have dwelt upon the speech which has been so graciously delivered from the throne today – to have gone into its details, and to have pointed out the many great and beneficial alterations and amendments in our existing institutions which it hints at and recommends to the House. The speech of last year was full of reforms in words, and in words only; but this speech contains the great leading features of all the salutary reforms the country wants; and if they are worked out fairly and honestly in detail, I am convinced the country will require no further amelioration of its institutions, and that it will become the envy and admiration of the world. I, therefore, hail the speech with great satisfaction.

It has been observed that the object of a king's speech is to say as little in as many words as possible; but this speech contains more things than words – it contains those great principles which, adopted in practice, will be most salutary not only to the British Empire, but to the world. When speaking of our foreign policy, it rejoices in the cooperation between France and this country; but it abstains from conveying any ministerial approbation of alterations in the domestic laws of that country which aim at the suppression of public liberty, and the checking of public discussion, such as call for individual reprobation, and which I reprobate as much as any one. I should like to know whether there is a statesman in the country who will get up in this House and avow his approval of such proceedings on the part of the French government. I know it may be done out of the House amid the cheers of an assembly of friends; but the government have, in my opinion, wisely abstained from reprobating such measures in the speech, while they have properly exulted in such a union of the two countries as will contribute to the national independence and the public liberty of Europe.

Years are coming over me, but my heart is as young and as ready as ever in the service of my country, of which I glory in being the pensionary and the hired advocate. I stand in a situation in which no man ever stood yet – the faithful friend of my country – its servant – its stave, if you will – I speak its sentiments by turns to you and to itself. I require no £20,000,000 on behalf of Ireland – I ask you only for justice: will you – can you – I will not say dare you refuse, because that would make you turn the other way. I implore you, as English gentlemen, to take this matter into consideration now, because you never had such an opportunity of conciliating. Experience makes fools wise; you are not fools, but you have yet to be convinced. I cannot forget the year 1825. We begged then as we would for a beggar's boon; we asked for emancipation by all that is sacred amongst us, and I remember how my speech and person were treated on the Treasury Bench, when I had no opportunity of reply. The other place turned us out and sent us back again, but we showed that justice was with us. The noble lord says the other place has declared the same sentiments with himself; but he could not use a worse argument. It is the very reason why we should acquiesce in the measure of reform, for we have no hope from that House – all our hopes are centred in this; and I am the living representative of those hopes. I have no other reason for adhering to the ministry than because they, the chosen representatives of the people of England, are anxiously determined to give the same measure of reform to Ireland as that which England has received. I have not fatigued myself, but the House, in coming forward upon this occasion. I may be laughed and sneered at by those who talk of my power; but what has created it but the injustice that has been done in Ireland? That is the end and the means of the magic, if you please – the groundwork of my influence in Ireland. If you refuse justice to that country, it is a melancholy consideration to me to think that you are adding substantially to that power and influence, while you are wounding my country to its very heart's core; weakening that throne, the monarch who sits upon which, you say you respect; severing that union which, you say, is bound together by the tightest links, and withholding that justice from Ireland which she will not cease to seek till it is obtained; every man must admit that the course I am taking is the legitimate and proper course – I defy any man to say it is not. Condemn me elsewhere as much as you please, but this you must admit. You may taunt the ministry with having coalesced me, you may raise the vulgar cry of "Irishman and Papist" against me, you may send out men called ministers of God to slander and calumniate me; they may assume whatever garb they please, but the question comes into this narrow compass. I demand, I respectfully insist: on equal justice for Ireland, on the same principle by which it has been administered to Scotland and England. I will not take less. Refuse me that if you can.

"ASK NOT WHAT YOUR COUNTRY CAN DO FOR YOU..." John F. Kennedy

On January 20, 1961, John F. Kennedy's inaugural speech as President of the USA lit a torch for a new generation. Its stirring phrases were designed to appeal to America's citizens' pride in their country, their fear of Communism, their religious beliefs and their sense of America being a force for justice around the world.

Vice President Johnson, Mr Speaker, Mr Chief Justice, President Eisenhower, Vice President Nixon, President Truman, Reverend Clergy, fellow citizens:

We observe today not a victory of party, but a celebration of freedom – symbolizing an end, as well as a beginning – signifying renewal, as well as change. For I have sworn before you and Almighty God the same solemn oath our forebears prescribed nearly a century and three-quarters ago.

The world is very different now. For man holds in his mortal hands the power to abolish all forms of human poverty and all forms of human life. And yet the same revolutionary beliefs for which our forebears fought are still at issue around the globe -- the belief that the rights of man come not from the generosity of the state, but from the hand of God.

We dare not forget today that we are the heirs of that first revolution. Let the word go forth from this time and place, to friend and foe alike, that the torch has been passed to a new generation of Americans – born in this century, tempered by war, disciplined by a hard and bitter peace, proud of our ancient heritage, and unwilling to witness or permit the slow undoing of those human rights to which this nation has always been committed, and to which we are committed today at home and around the world.

Let every nation know, whether it wishes us well or ill, that we shall pay any price, bear any burden, meet any hardship, support any friend, oppose any foe, to assure the survival and the success of liberty.

This much we pledge – and more.

To those old allies whose cultural and spiritual origins we share, we pledge the loyalty of faithful friends. United there is little we cannot do in a host of cooperative ventures. Divided there is little we can do – for we dare not meet a powerful challenge at odds and split asunder.

To those new states whom we welcome to the ranks of the free, we pledge our word that one form of colonial control shall not have passed away merely to be replaced by a far more iron tyranny. We shall not always expect to find them supporting our view. But we shall always hope to find them strongly supporting their own freedom – and to remember that, in the past, those who foolishly sought power by riding the back of the tiger ended up inside.

To those people in the huts and villages of half the globe struggling to break the bonds of mass misery, we pledge our best efforts to help them help themselves, for whatever period is required – not because the Communists may be doing it, not because we seek their votes, but because it is right. If a free society cannot help the many who are poor, it cannot save the few who are rich.

To our sister republics south of our border, we offer a special pledge: to convert our good words into good deeds, in a new alliance for progress, to assist free men and free governments in casting off the chains of poverty. But this peaceful revolution of hope cannot become the prey of hostile powers. Let all our neighbours know that we shall join with them to oppose aggression or subversion anywhere in the Americas. And let every other power know that this hemisphere intends to remain the master of its own house.

To that world assembly of sovereign states, the United Nations, our last best hope in an age where the instruments of war have far outpaced the instruments of peace, we renew our pledge of support – to prevent it from becoming merely a forum for invective, to strengthen its shield of the new and the weak, and to enlarge the area in which its writ may run.

Finally, to those nations who would make themselves our adversary, we offer not a pledge but a request: that both sides begin anew the quest for peace, before the dark powers of destruction unleashed by science engulf all humanity in planned or accidental self-destruction.

We dare not tempt them with weakness. For only when our arms are sufficient beyond doubt can we be certain beyond doubt that they will never be employed.

But neither can two great and powerful groups of nations take comfort from our present course – both sides overburdened by the cost of modern weapons, both rightly alarmed by the steady spread of the deadly atom, yet both racing to alter that uncertain balance of terror that stays the hand of mankind's final war.

So let us begin anew – remembering on both sides that civility is not a sign of weakness, and sincerity is always subject to proof. Let us never negotiate out of fear, but let us never fear to negotiate.

Let both sides explore what problems unite us instead of belabouring those problems which divide us.

Let both sides, for the first time, formulate serious and precise proposals for the inspection and control of arms, and bring the absolute power to destroy other nations under the absolute control of all nations.

Let both sides seek to invoke the wonders of science instead of its terrors. Together let us explore the stars, conquer the deserts, eradicate disease, tap the ocean depths, and encourage the arts and commerce.

Let both sides unite to heed, in all corners of the earth, the command of Isaiah – to "undo the heavy burdens, and let the oppressed go free".

And, if a beachhead of cooperation may push back the jungle of suspicion, let both sides join in creating a new endeavour – not a new balance of power, but a new world of law – where the strong are just, and the weak secure, and the peace preserved.

All this will not be finished in the first 100 days. Nor will it be finished in the first 1,000 days; nor in the life of this Administration; nor even perhaps in our lifetime on this planet. But let us begin.

In your hands, my fellow citizens, more than mine, will rest the final success or failure of our course. Since this country was founded, each generation of Americans has been summoned to give testimony to its national loyalty. The graves of young Americans who answered the call to service surround the globe.

Now the trumpet summons us again – not as a call to bear arms, though arms we need – not as a call to battle, though embattled we are – but a call to bear the burden of a long twilight struggle, year in and year out, "rejoicing in hope; patient in tribulation", a struggle against the common enemies of man: tyranny, poverty, disease, and war itself.

Can we forge against these enemies a grand and global alliance, North and South, East and West, that can assure a more fruitful life for all mankind? Will you join in that historic effort?

In the long history of the world, only a few generations have been granted the role of defending freedom in its hour of maximum danger. I do not shrink from this responsibility – I welcome it. I do not believe that any of us would exchange places with any other people or any other generation. The energy, the faith, the devotion which we bring to this endeavour will light our country and all who serve it. And the glow from that fire can truly light the world.

And so, my fellow Americans, ask not what your country can do for you; ask what you can do for your country.

My fellow citizens of the world, ask not what America will do for you, but what together we can do for the freedom of man.

Finally, whether you are citizens of America or citizens of the world, ask of us here the same high standards of strength and sacrifice which we ask of you. With a good conscience our only sure reward, with history the final judge of our deeds, let us go forth to lead the land we love, asking His blessing and His help, but knowing that here on earth God's work must truly be our own.

PHILOSOPHY

"THIS WORLD IS NOT PERFECT"
Dalai Lama

The 14th Dalai Lama went into exile from Tibet at the age of 12 in 1950. He has spent the years since campaigning for a degree of autonomy for his homeland and for oppressed peoples everywhere. His tireless optimism and message of nonviolence has won him admirers the world over.

The fact that there is always a positive side to life is the one thing that gives me a lot of happiness. This world is not perfect. There are problems. But things like happiness and unhappiness are relative. Realizing this gives you hope.

"OCCAM'S RAZOR"
William of Occam

The 13th-century English Franciscan friar Occam was put on trial for heresy for the statement below, which translates as "Plurality should not be assumed without necessity," which was seen as meaning that he doubted the existence of God. In effect, the fewer assumptions needed to explain something, the more likely the answer is to be correct. If there are two competing theories which make exactly the same predictions, the one that is simpler is the better.

Pluralitas non est ponenda sine necessitate.

"MEANS AND ENDS"
Niccolo Machiavelli

The name of the 15th-century Florentine public servant Machiavelli is now synonymous with the idea that for politicians and rulers the ends justify the means, however repellent the latter may be. In his pamphlet, *The Prince*, he expanded the theory.

Therefore it is unnecessary for a prince to have all the good qualities I have enumerated, but it is very necessary to appear to have them. And I shall dare to say this also, that to have them and always to observe them is injurious, and that to appear to have them is useful; to appear merciful, faithful, humane, religious, upright, and to be so, but with a mind so framed that should you require not to be so, you may be able and know how to change to the opposite.

And you have to understand this, that a prince, especially a new one, cannot observe all those things for which men are esteemed, being often forced, in order to maintain the state, to act contrary to fidelity, friendship, humanity and religion. Therefore it is necessary for him to have a mind ready to turn itself accordingly as the winds and variations of fortune force it, yet, as I have said above, not to diverge from the good if he can avoid doing so, but, if compelled, then to know how to set about it...

...a prince wishing to keep his state is very often forced to do evil.

"THE DICTATORSHIP OF THE PROLETARIAT"
Karl Marx

At an after-dinner speech at the launch of the *People's Post* in London in 1856, Marx spoke eloquently about the conditions imposed on the working classes by the industrial revolution and the urgent need for their emancipation.

The so-called revolutions of 1848 were but poor incidents – small fractures and fissures in the dry crust of European society.

However, they announced the abyss. Beneath the apparently solid surface, they betrayed oceans of liquid matter, only needing expansion to rend into fragments continents of hard rock. Noisedly and confusedly they proclaimed the emancipation of the proletarian, i.e. the secret of the 19th century, and of the revolution of that century.

That social revolution, it is true, was no novelty invented in 1848. Steam, electricity and the self-acting mule were revolutionists of a rather more dangerous character than even citizens Barbès, Raspail and Blanqui. But, although the atmosphere in which we live weighs upon everyone with a 20,000lb force, do you feel it? No more than European society before 1848 felt the revolutionary atmosphere enveloping and pressing it from all sides.

There is one great fact, characteristic of this, our 19th century, a fact which no party dares deny. On the one hand, there have started into life industrial and scientific forces which no epoch of the former human history had ever suspected. On the other hand, there exist symptoms of decay far surpassing the horrors recorded of the latter times of the Roman Empire. In our days everything seems pregnant with its contrary; machinery gifted with the wonderful power of shortening and fructifying human labour we behold starving and overworking it. The newfangled sources of wealth, by some strange, weird spell, are turned into sources of want. The victories of art seem bought by the loss of character.

At the same pace that mankind masters nature, man seems to become enslaved to other men or to his own infamy. Even the pure light of science seems unable to shine but on the dark background of ignorance. All our invention and progress seem to result in endowing material forces with intellectual life, and in stultifying human life into a material force.

This antagonism between modern industry and science on the one hand, modern misery and dissolution on the other hand; this antagonism between the productive powers and the social relations of our epoch is a fact, palpable, overwhelming and not to be controverted. Some parties may wail over it; others may wish to get rid of modern arts in order to get rid of modern conflicts. Or they may imagine that so signal a progress in industry wants to be completed by as signal a regress in politics.

On our part, we do not mistake the shape of the shrewd spirit that continues to mark all these contradictions. We know that to work well the newfangled forces of society, they only want to be mastered by newfangled men – and such are the workingmen. They are as much the invention of modern time as machinery itself. In the signs that bewilder the middle class, the aristocracy and the poor prophets of regression, we do recognize our brave friend Robin Goodfellow, the old mole, that can work in the earth so fast, that worthy pioneer – the revolution.

The English workingmen are the firstborn sons of modern industry. They will then, certainly, not be the last in aiding the social revolution produced by that industry, a revolution which means the emancipation of their own class all over the world, which is as universal as capital rule and wage slavery.

I know the heroic struggles the English working class have gone through since the middle of the last century – struggles less glorious because they are shrouded in obscurity and burked by the middle-class historians to revenge the misdeeds of the ruling class. There existed in the Middle Ages in Germany a secret tribunal called the *Vehmgericht*. If a red cross was seen marked on a house, people knew that its owner was doomed by the Vehm. All the houses of Europe are now marked with the mysterious red cross. History is the judge – its executioner, the proletarian.

HUMANITY & LIBERTY

"WE ACCEPT TO LIVE WITH YOU..."
Anwar el-Sadat

On November 19 and 20, 1977, the Egyptian president, Anwar el-Sadat, made an unprecedented visit to Jerusalem. Until then he had been an implacable foe of the state of Israel; his visit stunned the world and led to the Camp David Accords in 1979, in which, in return for peace, Israel returned the Sinai Peninsula to Egypt. Making peace with Israel isolated Egypt from the rest of the Arab world and President Sadat was assassinated by Egyptian soldiers in October 1981.

...today I tell you, and I declare it to the whole world, that we accept to live with you in permanent peace based on justice. We do not want to encircle you or be encircled ourselves by destructive missiles ready for launching, nor by the shells of grudges and hatreds.

I have announced on more than one occasion that Israel has become a *fait accompli*, recognized by the world, and that the two superpowers have undertaken the responsibility for its security and the defence of its existence. As we really and truly seek peace we really and truly welcome you to live among us in peace and security.

"UNIVERSAL DECLARATION OF HUMAN RIGHTS"
General Assembly of the United Nations

Resolution 217 A (III) was adopted by the General Assembly of the United Nations on December 10, 1948. Its 30 articles sought to define the fundamental rights of every person on the planet.

PREAMBLE
Whereas recognition of the inherent dignity and of the equal and inalienable rights of all members of the human family is the foundation of freedom, justice and peace in the world,

Whereas disregard and contempt for human rights have resulted in barbarous acts which have outraged the conscience of mankind, and the advent of a world in which human beings shall enjoy freedom of speech and belief and freedom from fear and want has been proclaimed as the highest aspiration of the common people,

Whereas it is essential, if man is not to be compelled to have recourse, as a last resort, to rebellion against tyranny and oppression, that human rights should be protected by the rule of law,

Whereas it is essential to promote the development of friendly relations between nations,

Whereas the peoples of the United Nations have in the Charter reaffirmed their faith in fundamental human rights, in the dignity and worth of the human person and in the equal rights of men and women and have determined to promote social progress and better standards of life in larger freedom,

Whereas Member States have pledged themselves to achieve, in cooperation with the United Nations, the promotion of universal respect for and observance of human rights and fundamental freedoms,

Whereas a common understanding of these rights and freedoms is of the greatest importance for the full realization of this pledge,

Now, therefore **THE GENERAL ASSEMBLY** proclaims **THIS UNIVERSAL DECLARATION OF HUMAN RIGHTS** as a common standard of achievement for all peoples and all nations, to the end that every individual and every organ of society, keeping this Declaration constantly in mind, shall strive by teaching and education to promote respect for these rights and freedoms and by progressive measures, national and international, to secure their universal and effective recognition and observance, both among the peoples of Member States themselves and among the peoples of territories under their jurisdiction.

Article 1.
All human beings are born free and equal in dignity and rights.They are endowed with reason and conscience and should act towards one another in a spirit of brotherhood.

Article 2.
Everyone is entitled to all the rights and freedoms set forth in this Declaration, without distinction of any kind, such as race, colour, sex, language, religion, political or other opinion, national or social origin, property, birth or other status. Furthermore, no distinction shall be made on the basis of the political, jurisdictional or international status of the country or territory to which a person belongs, whether it be independent, trust, non-self-governing or under any other limitation of sovereignty.

Article 3.
Everyone has the right to life, liberty and security of person.

Article 4.
No one shall be held in slavery or servitude; slavery and the slave

trade shall be prohibited in all their forms.

Article 5.
No one shall be subjected to torture or to cruel, inhuman or degrading treatment or punishment.

Article 6.
Everyone has the right to recognition everywhere as a person before the law.

Article 7.
All are equal before the law and are entitled without any discrimination to equal protection of the law. All are entitled to equal protection against any discrimination in violation of this Declaration and against any incitement to such discrimination.

Article 8.
Everyone has the right to an effective remedy by the competent national tribunals for acts violating the fundamental rights granted him by the constitution or by law.

Article 9.
No one shall be subjected to arbitrary arrest, detention or exile.

Article 10.
Everyone is entitled in full equality to a fair and public hearing by an independent and impartial tribunal, in the determination of his rights and obligations and of any criminal charge against him.

Article 11.
(1) Everyone charged with a penal offence has the right to be presumed innocent until proved guilty according to law in a public trial at which he has had all the guarantees necessary for his defence.
(2) No one shall be held guilty of any penal offence on account of any act or omission which did not constitute a penal offence, under national or international law, at the time when it was committed. Nor shall a heavier penalty be imposed than the one

that was applicable at the time the penal offence was committed.

Article 12.
No one shall be subjected to arbitrary interference with his privacy, family, home or correspondence, nor to attacks upon his honour and reputation. Everyone has the right to the protection of the law against such interference or attacks.

Article 13.
(1) Everyone has the right to freedom of movement and residence within the borders of each state.
(2) Everyone has the right to leave any country, including his own, and to return to his country.

Article 14.
(1) Everyone has the right to seek and to enjoy in other countries asylum from persecution.
(2) This right may not be invoked in the case of prosecutions genuinely arising from non-political crimes or from acts contrary to the purposes and principles of the United Nations.

Article 15.
(1) Everyone has the right to a nationality.
(2) No one shall be arbitrarily deprived of his nationality nor denied the right to change his nationality.

Article 16.
(1) Men and women of full age, without any limitation due to race, nationality or religion, have the right to marry and to found a family. They are entitled to equal rights as to marriage, during marriage and at its dissolution.
(2) Marriage shall be entered into only with the free and full consent of the intending spouses.
(3) The family is the natural and fundamental group unit of society and is entitled to protection by society and the State.

Article 17.
(1) Everyone has the right to own property alone as well as in

association with others.
(2) No one shall be arbitrarily deprived of his property.

Article 18.
Everyone has the right to freedom of thought, conscience and religion; this right includes freedom to change his religion or belief, and freedom, either alone or in community with others and in public or private, to manifest his religion or belief in teaching, practice, worship and observance.

Article 19.
Everyone has the right to freedom of opinion and expression; this right includes freedom to hold opinions without interference and to seek, receive and impart information and ideas through any media and regardless of frontiers.

Article 20.
(1) Everyone has the right to freedom of peaceful assembly and association.
(2) No one may be compelled to belong to an association.

Article 21.
(1) Everyone has the right to take part in the government of his country, directly or through freely chosen representatives.
(2) Everyone has the right of equal access to public service in his country.
(3) The will of the people shall be the basis of the authority of government; this will shall be expressed in periodic and genuine elections which shall be by universal and equal suffrage and shall be held by secret vote or by equivalent free voting procedures.

Article 22.
Everyone, as a member of society, has the right to social security and is entitled to realization, through national effort and international co-operation and in accordance with the organization and resources of each State, of the economic, social and cultural rights indispensable for his dignity and the free development of his personality.

Article 23.
(1) Everyone has the right to work, to free choice of employment, to just and favourable conditions of work and to protection against unemployment.
(2) Everyone, without any discrimination, has the right to equal pay for equal work.
(3) Everyone who works has the right to just and favourable remuneration ensuring for himself and his family an existence worthy of human dignity, and supplemented, if necessary, by other means of social protection.
(4) Everyone has the right to form and to join trade unions for the protection of his interests.

Article 24.
Everyone has the right to rest and leisure, including reasonable limitation of working hours and periodic holidays with pay.

Article 25.
(1) Everyone has the right to a standard of living adequate for the health and well-being of himself and of his family, including food, clothing, housing and medical care and necessary social services, and the right to security in the event of unemployment, sickness, disability, widowhood, old age or other lack of livelihood in circumstances beyond his control.
(2) Motherhood and childhood are entitled to special care and assistance. All children, whether born in or out of wedlock, shall enjoy the same social protection.

Article 26.
(1) Everyone has the right to education. Education shall be free, at least in the elementary and fundamental stages. Elementary education shall be compulsory. Technical and professional education shall be made generally available and higher education shall be equally accessible to all on the basis of merit.
(2) Education shall be directed to the full development of the human personality and to the strengthening of respect for human rights and fundamental freedoms. It shall promote understanding, tolerance and friendship among all nations, racial or religious

groups, and shall further the activities of the United Nations for the maintenance of peace.
(3) Parents have a prior right to choose the kind of education that shall be given to their children.

Article 27.
(1) Everyone has the right freely to participate in the cultural life of the community, to enjoy the arts and to share in scientific advancement and its benefits.
(2) Everyone has the right to the protection of the moral and material interests resulting from any scientific, literary or artistic production of which he is the author.

Article 28.
Everyone is entitled to a social and international order in which the rights and freedoms set forth in this Declaration can be fully realized.

Article 29.
(1) Everyone has duties to the community in which alone the free and full development of his personality is possible.
(2) In the exercise of his rights and freedoms, everyone shall be subject only to such limitations as are determined by law solely for the purpose of securing due recognition and respect for the rights and freedoms of others and of meeting the just requirements of morality, public order and the general welfare in a democratic society.
(3) These rights and freedoms may in no case be exercised contrary to the purposes and principles of the United Nations.

Article 30.
Nothing in this Declaration may be interpreted as implying for any State, group or person any right to engage in any activity or to perform any act aimed at the destruction of any of the rights and freedoms set forth herein.

"I HAVE A DREAM"
Martin Luther King

One of the most memorable speeches of the 20th century was delivered by the Revd Martin Luther King Jr, on the steps of the Lincoln Memorial in Washington DC on August 28, 1963.

Five score years ago, a great American, in whose symbolic shadow we stand signed the Emancipation Proclamation. This momentous decree came as a great beacon light of hope to millions of Negro slaves who had been seared in the flames of withering injustice. It came as a joyous daybreak to end the long night of captivity. But one hundred years later, we must face the tragic fact that the Negro is still not free.

One hundred years later, the life of the Negro is still sadly crippled by the manacles of segregation and the chains of discrimination. One hundred years later, the Negro lives on a lonely island of poverty in the midst of a vast ocean of material prosperity. One hundred years later, the Negro is still languishing in the corners of American society and finds himself an exile in his own land.

So we have come here today to dramatize an appalling condition. In a sense we have come to our nation's capital to cash a cheque. When the architects of our republic wrote the magnificent words of the Constitution and the Declaration of Independence, they were signing a promissory note to which every American was to fall heir.

This note was a promise that all men would be guaranteed the inalienable rights of life, liberty and the pursuit of happiness. It is obvious today that America has defaulted on this promissory note insofar as her citizens of colour are concerned. Instead of honouring this sacred obligation, America has given the Negro people a bad check which has come back marked "insufficient funds". But we refuse to believe that the bank of justice is bankrupt. We refuse to believe that there are insufficient funds in the great vaults of opportunity of this nation.

So we have come to cash this cheque – a cheque that will give us upon demand the riches of freedom and the security of justice. We have also come to this hallowed spot to remind America of the fierce urgency of now. This is no time to engage in the luxury of cooling off or to take the tranquillizing drug of gradualism. Now is the time to rise from the dark and desolate valley of segregation to the sunlit path of racial justice. Now is the time to open the doors of opportunity to all of God's children. Now is the time to lift our nation from the quicksands of racial injustice to the solid rock of brotherhood.

It would be fatal for the nation to overlook the urgency of the moment and to underestimate the determination of the Negro. This sweltering summer of the Negro's legitimate discontent will not pass until there is an invigorating autumn of freedom and equality. Nineteen sixty-three is not an end, but a beginning. Those who hope that the Negro needed to blow off steam and will now be content will have a rude awakening if the nation returns to business as usual. There will be neither rest nor tranquillity in America until the Negro is granted his citizenship rights.

The whirlwinds of revolt will continue to shake the foundations of our nation until the bright day of justice emerges. But there is something that I must say to my people who stand on the warm threshold which leads into the palace of justice. In the process of gaining our rightful place we must not be guilty of wrongful deeds. Let us not seek to satisfy our thirst for freedom by drinking from the cup of bitterness and hatred.

We must forever conduct our struggle on the high plane of dignity and discipline. We must not allow our creative protest to degenerate into physical violence. Again and again we must rise to the majestic heights of meeting physical force with soul force. The marvellous new militancy which has engulfed the Negro community must not lead us to distrust of all white people, for many of our white brothers, as evidenced by their presence here today, have come to realize that their destiny is tied up with our destiny and their freedom is inextricably bound to our freedom.

We cannot walk alone. And as we walk, we must make the pledge that we shall march ahead. We cannot turn back. There are those who are asking the devotees of civil rights, “When will you be satisfied?” We can never be satisfied as long as our bodies, heavy with the fatigue of travel, cannot gain lodging in the motels of the highways and the hotels of the cities. We cannot be satisfied as long as the Negro’s basic mobility is from a smaller ghetto to a larger one. We can never be satisfied as long as a Negro in Mississippi cannot vote and a Negro in New York believes he has nothing for which to vote. No, no, we are not satisfied, and we will not be satisfied until justice rolls down like waters and righteousness like a mighty stream.

I am not unmindful that some of you have come here out of great trials and tribulations. Some of you have come fresh from narrow cells. Some of you have come from areas where your quest for freedom left you battered by the storms of persecution and staggered by the winds of police brutality. You have been the veterans of creative suffering. Continue to work with the faith that unearned suffering is redemptive.

Go back to Mississippi, go back to Alabama, go back to Georgia, go back to Louisiana, go back to the slums and ghettos of our northern cities, knowing that somehow this situation can and will be changed. Let us not wallow in the valley of despair. I say to you today, my friends, that in spite of the difficulties and frustrations of the moment, I still have a dream. It is a dream deeply rooted in the American dream.

I have a dream that one day this nation will rise up and live out the true meaning of its creed: “We hold these truths to be self-evident: that all men are created equal.” I have a dream that one day on the red hills of Georgia the sons of former slaves and the sons of former slaveowners will be able to sit down together at a table of brotherhood. I have a dream that one day even the state of Mississippi, a desert state, sweltering with the heat of injustice and oppression, will be transformed into an oasis of freedom and justice. I have a dream that my four children will one day live in a nation where they will not be judged by the colour of their skin but by the content of their character. I have a dream today.

I have a dream that one day the state of Alabama, whose governor's lips are presently dripping with the words of interposition and nullification, will be transformed into a situation where little black boys and black girls will be able to join hands with little white boys and white girls and walk together as sisters and brothers. I have a dream today. I have a dream that one day every valley shall be exalted, every hill and mountain shall be made low, the rough places will be made plain, and the crooked places will be made straight, and the glory of the Lord shall be revealed, and all flesh shall see it together. This is our hope. This is the faith with which I return to the South. With this faith we will be able to hew out of the mountain of despair a stone of hope. With this faith we will be able to transform the jangling discords of our nation into a beautiful symphony of brotherhood. With this faith we will be able to work together, to pray together, to struggle together, to go to jail together, to stand up for freedom together, knowing that we will be free one day.

This will be the day when all of God's children will be able to sing with a new meaning, "My country, 'tis of thee, sweet land of liberty, of thee I sing. Land where my fathers died, land of the pilgrim's pride, from every mountainside, let freedom ring." And if America is to be a great nation, this must become true. So let freedom ring from the prodigious hilltops of New Hampshire. Let freedom ring from the mighty mountains of New York. Let freedom ring from the heightening Alleghenies of Pennsylvania! Let freedom ring from the snowcapped Rockies of Colorado! Let freedom ring from the curvaceous peaks of California! But not only that; let freedom ring from Stone Mountain of Georgia! Let freedom ring from Lookout Mountain of Tennessee! Let freedom ring from every hill and every molehill of Mississippi. From every mountainside, let freedom ring.

When we let freedom ring, when we let it ring from every village and every hamlet, from every state and every city, we will be able to speed up that day when all of God's children, black men and white men, Jews and Gentiles, Protestants and Catholics, will be able to join hands and sing in the words of the old Negro spiritual, "Free at last! Free at last! Thank God Almighty, we are free at last!"

"ON WOMEN'S RIGHT TO VOTE"
Susan B. Anthony

In the 19th century women in many countries did not have the right to vote. American suffragist Susan B. Anthony gave this rousing speech after her arrest for casting an illegal vote in the presidential election of 1872.

Friends and fellow citizens: I stand before you tonight under indictment for the alleged crime of having voted at the last presidential election, without having a lawful right to vote. It shall be my work this evening to prove to you that in thus voting, I not only committed no crime, but, instead, simply exercised my citizen's rights, guaranteed to me and all United States citizens by the National Constitution, beyond the power of any state to deny.

The preamble of the Federal Constitution says:

"We, the people of the United States, in order to form a more perfect union, establish justice, ensure domestic tranquillity, provide for the common defence, promote the general welfare, and secure the blessings of liberty to ourselves and our posterity, do ordain and establish this Constitution for the United States of America."

It was we, the people; not we, the white male citizens; nor yet we, the male citizens; but we, the whole people, who formed the Union. And we formed it, not to give the blessings of liberty, but to secure them; not to the half of ourselves and the half of our posterity, but to the whole people – women as well as men. And it is a downright mockery to talk to women of their enjoyment of the blessings of liberty while they are denied the use of the only means of securing them provided by this democratic-republican government – the ballot.

For any state to make sex a qualification that must ever result in the disfranchisement of one entire half of the people, is to pass a bill of attainder, or, an *ex post facto* law, and is therefore a violation of the supreme law of the land. By it the blessings of liberty are forever withheld from women and their female posterity.

To them this government has no just powers derived from the consent of the governed. To them this government is not a democracy. It is not a republic. It is an odious aristocracy; a hateful oligarchy of sex; the most hateful aristocracy ever established on the face of the globe; an oligarchy of wealth, where the rich govern the poor. An oligarchy of learning, where the educated govern the ignorant, or even an oligarchy of race, where the Saxon rules the African, might be endured; but this oligarchy of sex, which makes father, brothers, husband, sons, the oligarchs over the mother and sisters, the wife and daughters, of every household – which ordains all men sovereigns, all women subjects, carries dissension, discord, and rebellion into every home of the nation.

Webster, Worcester, and Bouvier all define a citizen to be a person in the United States, entitled to vote and hold office.

The only question left to be settled now is: Are women persons? And I hardly believe any of our opponents will have the hardihood to say they are not. Being persons, then, women are citizens; and no state has a right to make any law, or to enforce any old law, that shall abridge their privileges or immunities. Hence, every discrimination against women in the constitutions and laws of the several states is today null and void, precisely as is every one against Negroes.

"GIVE ME LIBERTY OR GIVE ME DEATH"
Patrick Henry

On March 23, 1775 Virginian Patrick Henry stood up in the Continental Congress in Richmond, Virginia. After hearing a series of resolutions about the defence of American civil rights and liberties he made the following speech, which Thomas Jefferson later claimed started the revolution in Virginia.

No man thinks more highly than I do of the patriotism, as well as abilities, of the very worthy gentlemen who have just addressed the House. But different men often see the same subject in different lights; and, therefore, I hope it will not be thought disrespectful to those gentlemen if, entertaining as I do opinions of a character very opposite to theirs, I shall speak forth my sentiments freely and without reserve. This is no time for ceremony. The questing before the House is one of awful moment to this country. For my own part, I consider it as nothing less than a question of freedom or slavery; and in proportion to the magnitude of the subject ought to be the freedom of the debate. It is only in this way that we can hope to arrive at truth, and fulfil the great responsibility which we hold to God and our country. Should I keep back my opinions at such a time, through fear of giving offence, I should consider myself as guilty of treason towards my country, and of an act of disloyalty toward the Majesty of Heaven, which I revere above all earthly kings.

Mr President, it is natural to man to indulge in the illusions of hope. We are apt to shut our eyes against a painful truth, and listen to the song of that siren till she transforms us into beasts. Is this the part of wise men, engaged in a great and arduous struggle for liberty? Are we disposed to be of the number of those who, having eyes, see not and, having ears, hear not the things which so nearly concern their temporal salvation? For my part, whatever anguish of spirit it may cost, I am willing to know the whole truth; to know the worst, and to provide for it.

I have but one lamp by which my feet are guided, and that is the lamp of experience. I know of no way of judging of the future but by the past. And judging by the past, I wish to know what there has been in the conduct of the British ministry for the last ten years to justify those hopes with which gentlemen have been pleased to solace themselves and the House. Is it that insidious smile with which our petition has been lately received? Trust it not, sir; it will prove a snare to your feet. Suffer not yourselves to be betrayed with a kiss. Ask yourselves how this gracious reception of our petition comports with those warlike preparations which cover our waters and darken our land. Are fleets and armies necessary to a work of love and reconciliation? Have we shown ourselves so unwilling to be reconciled that force must be called in to win back our love? Let us not deceive ourselves, sir. These are the implements of war and subjugation; the last arguments to which kings resort. I ask gentlemen, sir, what means this martial array, if its purpose be not to force us to submission? Can gentlemen assign any other possible motive for it? Has Great Britain any enemy, in this quarter of the world, to call for all this accumulation of navies and armies? No, sir, she has none. They are meant for us: they can be meant for no other. They are sent over to bind and rivet upon us those chains which the British ministry have been so long forging. And what have we to oppose to them? Shall we try argument? Sir, we have been trying that for the last ten years. Have we anything new to offer upon the subject? Nothing. We have held the subject up in every light of which it is capable; but it has been all in vain. Shall we resort to entreaty and humble supplication? What terms shall we find which have not been already exhausted? Let us not, I beseech you, sir, deceive ourselves. Sir, we have done everything that could be done to avert the storm which is now coming on. We have petitioned; we have remonstrated; we have supplicated; we have prostrated ourselves before the throne, and have implored its interposition to arrest the tyrannical hands of the ministry and Parliament. Our petitions have been slighted; our remonstrances have produced additional violence and insult; our supplications have been disregarded; and we have been spurned, with contempt, from the foot of the throne! In vain, after these things, may we indulge the fond hope of peace and reconciliation. There is no longer any room for hope. If we wish to be free – if we mean to preserve inviolate those inestimable privileges for which we have been so long contending – if we mean not basely to abandon the noble struggle in which we have been so long engaged, and which we have pledged ourselves never to abandon until the glorious object of our contest shall be obtained – we must fight! I repeat it, sir, we must fight! An appeal to arms and to the God of hosts is all that is left us!

They tell us, sir, that we are weak; unable to cope with so formidable an adversary. But when shall we be stronger? Will it be the next week, or the next year? Will it be when we are totally disarmed, and when a British guard shall be stationed in every house? Shall we gather strength by irresolution and inaction? Shall we acquire the means of effectual resistance by lying supinely on our backs and hugging the delusive phantom of hope, until our enemies shall have bound us hand and foot? Sir, we are not weak if we make a proper use of those means which the God of nature hath placed in our power. The millions of people, armed in the holy cause of liberty, and in such a country as that which we possess, are invincible by any force which our enemy can send against us. Besides, sir, we shall not fight our battles alone. There is a just God who presides over the destinies of nations, and who will raise up friends to fight our battles for us. The battle, sir, is not to the strong alone; it is to the vigilant, the active, the brave. Besides, sir, we have no election. If we were base enough to desire it, it is now too late to retire from the contest. There is no retreat but in submission and slavery! Our chains are forged! Their clanking may be heard on the plains of Boston! The war is inevitable – and let it come! I repeat it, sir, let it come.

It is in vain, sir, to extenuate the matter. Gentlemen may cry, Peace, Peace – but there is no peace. The war is actually begun! The next gale that sweeps from the north will bring to our ears the clash of resounding arms! Our brethren are already in the field! Why stand we here idle? What is it that gentlemen wish? What would they have? Is life so dear, or peace so sweet, as to be purchased at the price of chains and slavery? Forbid it, Almighty God! I know not what course others may take; but as for me, give me liberty or give me death!

"GIVE ME THE ****ING MONEY"
Bob Geldof

On July 13, 1985, the massive Live Aid multi-venue concerts took place with the aim of raising funds for people starving because of wars in Ethiopia and the resulting famine. Frustrated at one presenter's apparent complacency, Geldof exploded and, thumping the table, pleaded with the audience:

Don't go to the pub tonight. There are people dying, *now*! So please, stay in and give me the ****ing money.

"HIS SOUL GOES MARCHING ON..."
John Brown

On November 2, 1859, the abolitionist John Brown was tried and found guilty of murder in Charles Town, Virginia. Earlier in the year he had seized the town of Harper's Ferry in order to liberate slaves, killing several citizens in the process. Many people believe that the incident at Harper's Ferry was the real beginning of the fight for the emancipation of slaves in America. Just a few years later, the Union soldiers' marching song, to the tune of the "Battle Hymn of the Republic", included the verse:

> **John Brown died that the slaves might be free,**
> **John Brown died that the slaves might be free,**
> **His soul goes marching on.**

I have, may it please the court, a few words to say. In the first place, I deny everything but what I have all along admitted – the design on my part to free the slaves. I intended certainly to have made a clean thing of that matter, as I did last winter when I went into Missouri and there took slaves without the snapping of a gun on either side, moved them through the country, and finally left them in Canada. I designed to have done the same thing again on a larger scale. That was all I intended. I never did intend murder, or treason, or the destruction of property, or to excite or incite slaves to rebellion, or to make insurrection.

I have another objection; and that is, it is unjust that I should suffer such a penalty. Had I interfered in the manner which I admit, and which I admit has been fairly proved (for I admire the truthfulness and candor of the greater portion of the witnesses who have testified in this case) – had I so interfered in behalf of the rich, the powerful, the intelligent, the so-called great, or in behalf of any of their friends – either father, mother, brother, sister, wife, or children, or any of that class – and suffered and sacrificed what I have in this interference, it would have been all right; and every man in this court would have deemed it an act worthy of reward rather than punishment.

This court acknowledges, as I suppose, the validity of the law of God. I see a book kissed here which I suppose to be the Bible, or at least the New Testament. That teaches me that all things whatsoever I would that men should do to me, I should do even so to them. It teaches me, further, to "remember them that are in bonds, as bound with them". I endeavoured to act up to that instruction. I say I am yet too young to understand that God is any respecter of persons. I believe that to have interfered as I have done – as I have always freely admitted I have done – in behalf of His despised poor was not wrong, but right. Now, if it is deemed necessary that I should forfeit my life for the furtherance of the ends of justice, and mingle my blood further with the blood of my children and with the blood of millions in this slave country whose rights are disregarded by wicked, cruel, and unjust enactments – I submit; so let it be done!

Let me say one word further.

I feel entirely satisfied with the treatment I have received on my trial. Considering all the circumstances it has been more generous than I expected. But I feel no consciousness of guilt. I have stated that from the first what was my intention and what was not. I never had any design against the life of any person, nor any disposition to commit treason, or excite slaves to rebel, or make any general insurrection. I never encouraged any man to do so, but always discouraged any idea of that kind.

Let me say also a word in regard to the statements made by some of those connected with me. I hear it has been stated by some of them that I have induced them to join me. But the contrary is true. I do not say this to injure them, but as regretting their weakness. There is not one of them but joined me of his own accord, and the greater part of them at their own expense. A number of them I never saw, and never had a word of conversation with till the day they came to me; and that was for the purpose I have stated.

Now I have done.

"MILITANT SUFFRAGISTS"
Emmeline Pankhurst

Emmeline Pankhurst was the leader of the "Suffragettes" in Britain in the late 19th and early 20th centuries, at a time when women in most countries had no voting rights and married women could not own their own property. Mrs Pankhurst gave this speech in Hartford, Connecticut, in 1913.

I do not come here as an advocate, because whatever position the suffrage movement may occupy in the United States of America, in England it has passed beyond the realm of advocacy and it has entered into the sphere of practical politics.

It has become the subject of revolution and civil war, and so tonight I am not here to advocate woman suffrage.

American suffragists can do that very well for themselves. I am here as a soldier who has temporarily left the field of battle in order to explain – it seems strange it should have to be explained – what civil war is like when civil war is waged by women.

I am not only here as a soldier temporarily absent from the field of battle; I am here – and that, I think, is the strangest part of my coming – I am here as a person who, according to the law courts of my country, it has been decided, is of no value to the community at all; and I am adjudged because of my life to be a dangerous person, under sentence of penal servitude in a convict prison.

So you see there is some special interest in hearing so unusual a person address you. I dare say, in the minds of many of you, you will perhaps forgive me this personal touch that I do not look either very like a soldier or very like a convict, and yet I am both.

It would take too long to trace the course of militant methods as adopted by women, because it is about eight years since the word militant was first used to describe what we were doing; it is about eight years since the first militant action was taken by women.

It was not militant at all, except that it provoked militancy on the part of those who were opposed to it.

When women asked questions in political meetings, and failed to get answers, they were not doing anything militant. To ask questions at political meetings is an acknowledged right of all people who attend public meetings; certainly in my country, men have always done it, and I hope they do it in America, because it seems to me that if you allow people to enter your legislatures without asking them any questions as to what they are going to do when they get there you are not exercising your citizen's rights and your citizen's duties as you ought.

At any rate in Great Britain it is a custom, a time-honoured one, to ask questions of candidates for Parliament and ask questions of members of the government.

No man was ever put out of a public meeting for asking a question until Votes for Women came on to the political horizon.

The first people who were put out of a political meeting for asking questions were women; they were brutally ill-used; they found themselves in jail before twenty-four hours had expired.

But instead of the newspapers, which are largely inspired by the politicians, putting militancy and the reproach of militancy, if reproach there is, on the people who had assaulted the women, they actually said it was the women who were militant and very much to blame.

It was not the speakers on the platform, who would not answer them, who were to blame, or the ushers at the meeting; it was the poor women who had had their bruises and their knocks and scratches, and who were put into prison for doing precisely nothing but holding a protest meeting in the street after it was all over.

However, we were called militant for doing that, and we were quite willing to accept the name, because militancy for us is time-honoured; you have the church militant and in the sense of spiritual militancy we were very militant indeed.

We were determined to press this question of the enfranchisement of women to the point where we were no longer to be ignored by the politicians as had been the case for about fifty years, during which time women had patiently used every means open to them to win their political enfranchisement.

Experience will show you that if you really want to get anything done, it is not so much a matter of whether you alienate sympathy; sympathy is a very unsatisfactory thing if it is not practical sympathy.

It does not matter to the practical suffragist whether she alienates sympathy that was never of any use to her.

What she wants is to get something practical done, and whether it is done out of sympathy or whether it is done out of fear, or whether it is done because you want to be comfortable again and not be worried in this way, doesn't particularly matter so long as you get it.

We had enough of sympathy for fifty years; it never brought us anything; and we would rather have an angry man going to the government and saying, my business is interfered with and I won't submit to its being interfered with any longer because you won t give women the vote, than to have a gentleman come on to our platforms year in and year out and talk about his ardent sympathy with woman suffrage.

"Put them in prison,'" they said; "that will stop it." But it didn't stop it.

They put women in prison for long terms of imprisonment, for making a nuisance of themselves that was the expression when they took petitions in their hands to the door of the House of Commons; and they thought that by sending them to prison, giving them a day's imprisonment, would cause them all to settle down again and there would be no further trouble.

But it didn t happen so at all: instead of the women giving it up, more women did it, and more and more and more women did it until there were three hundred women at a time, who had not broken a single law, only 'made a nuisance of themselves' as the politicians say.

The whole argument with the anti-suffragists, or even the critical suffragist man, is this: that you can govern human beings without their consent.

They have said to us, "Government rests upon force; the women haven't force, so they must submit." Well, we are showing them that government does not rest upon force at all; it rests upon consent.

As long as women consent to be unjustly governed, they can be; but directly women say: "We withhold our consent, we will not be governed any longer so long as that government is unjust," not by the forces of civil war can you govern the very weakest woman.

You can kill that woman, but she escapes you then; you cannot govern her.

And that is, I think, a most valuable demonstration we have been making to the world. Now, I want to say to you who think women cannot succeed, we have brought the government of England to this position, that it has to face this alternative; either women are to be killed or women are to have the vote.

I ask American men in this meeting, what would you say if in your State you were faced with that alternative, that you must either kill them or give them their citizenship, women, many of whom you respect, women whom you know have lived useful lives, women whom you know, even if you do not know them personally, are animated with the highest motives, women who are in pursuit of liberty and the power to do useful public service?

Well, there is only one answer to that alternative; there is only one way out of it, unless you are prepared to put back civilization two or three generations; you must give those women the vote.

Now that is the outcome of our civil war.

You won your freedom in America when you had the Revolution, by bloodshed, by sacrificing human life.

You won the Civil War by the sacrifice of human life when you decided to emancipate the Negro.

You have left it to the women in your land, the men of all civilized countries have left it to women, to work out their own salvation.

That is the way in which we women of England are doing it.

Human life for us is sacred, but we say if any life is to be sacrificed it shall be ours; we won't do it ourselves, but we will put the enemy in the position where they will have to choose between giving us freedom or giving us death.

"AN IDEAL FOR WHICH I AM PREPARED TO DIE"
Nelson Mandela

In 1962, Nelson Mandela was arrested by South African security police for his opposition to the South African government's policies of discrimination against the nonwhite majority. In 1964, the government brought further charges of sabotage, high treason and conspiracy against him. This is part of Mandela's statement from the dock at his trial on April 20, 1964.

...In 1960 there was the shooting at Sharpeville, which resulted in the proclamation of a state of emergency and the declaration of the ANC as an unlawful organization. My colleagues and I, after careful consideration, decided that we would not obey this decree. The African people were not part of the Government and did not make the laws by which they were governed. We believed in the words of the Universal Declaration of Human Rights, that "the will of the people shall be the basis of authority of the Government," and for us to accept the banning was equivalent to accepting the silencing of the Africans for all time. The ANC refused to dissolve, but instead went underground. We believed it was our duty to preserve this organization which had been built up with almost fifty years of unremitting toil. I have no doubt that no self-respecting white political organization would disband itself if declared illegal by a government in which it had no say.

In 1960 the Government held a referendum which led to the establishment of the Republic. Africans, who constituted approximately 70 per cent of the population of South Africa, were not entitled to vote, and were not even consulted about the proposed constitutional change. All of us were apprehensive of our future under the proposed white Republic, and a resolution was taken to hold an All-in African Conference to call for a National Convention, and to organize mass demonstrations on the eve of the unwanted Republic, if the Government failed to call the Convention. The conference was attended by Africans of various political persuasions. I was the Secretary of the conference and undertook to be responsible for organizing the national stay-at-home which was subsequently called to coincide with the declaration of the Republic. As all strikes by Africans are illegal, the person organizing such a strike must avoid arrest. I was chosen to be this person, and consequently I had to leave my home and family and my practice and go into hiding to avoid arrest.

At the beginning of June 1961, after a long and anxious assessment of the South African situation, I, and some colleagues, came to the conclusion that as violence in this country was inevitable, it would be unrealistic and wrong for African leaders to continue preaching peace and nonviolence at a time when the Government met our peaceful demands with force...

...South Africa is the richest country in Africa, and could be one of the richest countries in the world. But it is a land of extremes and remarkable contrasts. The whites enjoy what may well be the highest standard of living in the world, whilst Africans live in poverty and misery. Forty per cent of the Africans live in hopelessly overcrowded and, in some cases, drought-stricken Reserves, where soil erosion and the overworking of the soil make it impossible for them to live properly off the land. Thirty per cent are labourers, labour tenants, and squatters on white farms and work and live under conditions similar to those of the serfs of the Middle Ages. The other 30 per cent live in towns where they have developed economic and social habits which bring them closer in many respects to white standards. Yet most Africans, even in this group, are impoverished by low incomes and high cost of living.

The complaint of Africans, however, is not only that they are poor and the whites are rich, but that the laws which are made by the whites are designed to preserve this situation. There are two ways to break out of poverty. The first is by formal education, and the second is by the worker acquiring a greater skill at his work and thus higher wages. As far as Africans are concerned, both these avenues of advancement are deliberately curtailed by legislation.

During my lifetime I have dedicated myself to this struggle of the African people. I have fought against white domination, and I have fought against black domination. I have cherished the ideal of a democratic and free society in which all persons live together in harmony and with equal opportunities. It is an ideal which I hope to live for and to achieve. But if needs be, it is an ideal for which I am prepared to die.

"THE OSLO ACCORDS"
Yitzhak Rabin and Yasser Arafat

On the White House lawn on September 13, 1993, Israeli Foreign Minister Shimon Peres and PLO Executive Council member Mahmud Abbas signed the historic first Israel-Palestinian agreement commonly known as the Oslo Accords.

Prime Minister Rabin
We say to you today in a loud and a clear voice: Enough of blood and tears. Enough. We have no desire for revenge. We harbour no hatred towards you. We, like you, are people who want to build a home, to plant a tree, to love, to live side by side with you in dignity, in empathy, as human beings, as free men. We are today giving peace a chance, and saying again to you: Enough. Let us pray that a day will come when we all will say: Farewell to the arms...

...To every thing there is a season, and a time to every purpose under heaven: A time to be born, and a time to die; A time to kill, and a time to heal; A time to weep and a time to laugh; A time to love, and a time to hate; A time of war, and a time of peace.

Ladies and Gentlemen, the time for peace has come.

Chairman Arafat
We will need more courage and determination to continue the course of building coexistence and peace between us. This is possible. And it will happen with mutual determination and with the effort that will be made with all parties on all the tracks to establish the foundations of a just and comprehensive peace. Our people do not consider that exercising the right to self-determination could violate the rights of their neighbours or

infringe on their security. Rather, putting an end to their feelings of being wronged and of having suffered an historic injustice is the strongest guarantee to achieve coexistence and openness between our two peoples and future generations.

"OUR LADY OF JASNA GÓRA"
Pope John Paul II

At the Jasna Góra monastery at Częstochowa in Poland on June 18, 1983, Pope John Paul II delivered a highly coded speech to a crowd of up to a million of his young compatriots. Many onlookers afterwards felt that the support expressed by the Pope gave the Polish people the heart they needed to break away from their Communist rulers.

...Before the Mother of Jasna Góra I wish to give thanks for all the proofs of this solidarity which have been given by my compatriots, including Polish youth, in the difficult period of not many months ago...

...My dear young friends! Before our common Mother and the Queen of our hearts, I desire finally to say to you that she knows your sufferings, your difficult youth, your sense of injustice and humiliation, the lack of prospects for the future that is so often felt, perhaps the temptations to flee to some other world... Because the way out in whatever dimension – economic, social, political – must happen first in man. Man cannot remain with no way out.

"THE DESTRUCTIVE MALE"
Elizabeth Cady Stanton

Elizabeth Cady Stanton helped to launch the women's rights movement in America in the 1840s. She gave this speech in 1868 at the Women's Suffrage Convention in Washington DC Stanton campaigned for more than 50 years for voting rights for American women and against the sexist social and political norms of her day.

I urge a 16th amendment, because "manhood suffrage", or a man's government, is civil, religious, and social disorganization. The male element is a destructive force, stern, selfish, aggrandizing, loving war, violence, conquest, acquisition, breeding in the material and moral world alike, discord, disorder, disease, and death. See what a record of blood and cruelty the pages of history reveal! Through what slavery, slaughter and sacrifice, through what inquisitions and imprisonments, pains and persecutions, black codes and gloomy creeds, the soul of humanity has struggled for centuries, while mercy has veiled her face and all hearts have been dead alike to love and hope!

The male element has held high carnival thus far; it has fairly run riot from the beginning, overpowering the feminine element everywhere, crushing out all the diviner qualities in human nature, until we know but little of true manhood and womanhood, of the latter comparatively nothing, for it has scarce been recognized as a power until within the last century. Society is but the reflection of man himself, untempered by woman's thought; the hard iron rule we feel alike in the church, the state and the home. No one need wonder at the disorganization, at the fragmentary condition of everything, when we remember that man, who represents but half a complete being, with but half an idea on every subject, has undertaken the absolute control of all sublunary matters.

People object to the demands of those whom they choose to call the strong-minded, because they say "the right of suffrage will make the women masculine". That is just the difficulty in which we are involved today. Though disfranchized, we have few women in the best sense; we have simply so many reflections, varieties and dilutions of the masculine gender. The strong, natural characteristics of womanhood are repressed and ignored in dependence, for so long as man feeds woman she will try to please the giver and adapt herself to his condition. To keep a foothold in society, woman must be as near like man as possible, reflect his ideas, opinions, virtues, motives, prejudices and vices. She must respect his statutes, though they strip her of every inalienable right and conflict with that higher law written by the finger of God on her own soul.

She must look at everything from its dollar-and-cent point of view, or she is a mere romancer. She must accept things as they are and make the best of them. To mourn over the miseries of others, the poverty of the poor, their hardships in jails, prisons, asylums, the horrors of war, cruelty, and brutality in every form, all this would be mere sentimentalizing. To protest against the intrigue, bribery, and corruption of public life, to desire that her sons might follow some business that did not involve lying, cheating and a hard, grinding selfishness would be arrant nonsense.

In this way man has been moulding woman to his ideas by direct and positive influences, while she, if not a negation, has used indirect means to control him, and in most cases developed the very characteristics both in him and herself that needed repression. And now man himself stands appalled at the results of his own excesses, and mourns in bitterness that falsehood, selfishness and violence are the law of life. The need of this hour is not territory, gold mines, railroads or specie payments but a new evangel of womanhood, to exalt purity, virtue, morality, true religion, to lift man up into the higher realms of thought and action.

We ask woman's enfranchisement, as the first step toward the recognition of that essential element in government that can only secure the health, strength and prosperity of the nation. Whatever is done to lift woman to her true position will help to usher in a new day of peace and perfection for the race.

In speaking of the masculine element, I do not wish to be understood to say that all men are hard, selfish and brutal, for many of the most beautiful spirits the world has known have been clothed with manhood; but I refer to those characteristics, though often marked in woman, that distinguish what is called the stronger sex. For example, the love of acquisition and conquest, the very pioneers of civilization, when expended on the earth, the sea, the elements, the riches and forces of nature, are powers of destruction when used to subjugate one man to another or to sacrifice nations to ambition.

Here that great conservator of woman's love, if permitted to assert itself, as it naturally would in freedom against oppression, violence and war, would hold all these destructive forces in check, for woman knows the cost of life better than man does, and not with her consent would one drop of blood ever be shed, one life sacrificed in vain.

With violence and disturbance in the natural world, we see a constant effort to maintain an equilibrium of forces. Nature, like a loving mother, is ever trying to keep land and sea, mountain and valley each in its place, to hush the angry winds and waves, balance the extremes of heat and cold, of rain and drought, that peace, harmony, and beauty may reign supreme. There is a striking analogy between matter and mind, and the present disorganization of society warns us that in the dethronement of woman we have let loose the elements of violence and ruin that she only has the power to curb. If the civilization of the age calls for an extension of the suffrage, surely a government of the most virtuous educated men and women would better represent the whole and protect the interests of all than could the representation of either sex alone.

"ADDRESS AT THE OPENING OF THE SOUTH AFRICAN PARLIAMENT, FEBRUARY 2, 1990"

F.W. de Klerk

Years of international and domestic pressure finally persuaded the South African government to abandon white minority rule. President de Klerk surprised many onlookers by announcing the unbanning of organizations like the African National Congress and the release of detainees held for belonging to such groups.

The agenda is open and the overall aims to which we are aspiring should be acceptable to all reasonable South Africans.

Among other things, those aims include a new, democratic constitution; universal franchise; no domination; equality before an independent judiciary; the protection of minorities as well as of individual rights; freedom of religion...dynamic programmes directed at better education, health services, housing and social conditions for all.

In this connection Mr Nelson Mandela could play an important part. The Government has noted that he has declared himself to be willing to make a constructive contribution to the peaceful political process in South Africa.

I wish to put it plainly that the Goverment has taken a firm decision to release Mr Mandela unconditionally...

"MARCH TO FREEDOM"
Nelson Mandela

Nine days after President de Klerk's announcement of his imminent release, Nelson Mandela was released from prison and addressed a rally of his supporters in Cape Town. After thanking the organizations and people who had supported the struggle against apartheid, he issued a clarion call to a final effort to end the injustices of the system.

Our struggle has reached a decisive moment. We call on our people to seize this moment, so that the process toward democracy is rapid and uninterrupted.

We have waited too long for our freedom. We can no longer wait. Now is the time to intensify the struggle on all fronts. To relax our efforts now would be a mistake which generations to come will not be able to forgive.

The sight of freedom looming on the horizon should encourage us to redouble our efforts. It is only through disciplined mass action that our victory can be assured.

We call on our white compatriots to join us in the shaping of a new South Africa. The freedom movement is a political home for you, too.

We call on the international community to continue the campaign to isolate the apartheid regime. To lift sanctions now would run the risk of aborting the process toward the complete eradication of apartheid.

Our march toward freedom is irreversible. We must not allow fear to stand in our way.

SPORT

"THE ASHES"
Reginald Brooks

In August 1882, the Australian cricket team did the unthinkable and beat the English team, in England. *The Times* newspaper the next day printed the following mock obituary. The contest between the two teams has been one of the most keenly fought ever since.

In Affectionate Remembrance of English Cricket Which Died At The Oval on 29th August 1882
Deeply lamented by a large circle of sorrowing friends and acquaintances
R.I.P
NB: The body will be cremated, and the ashes taken to Australia.

“I AM THE GREATEST” Muhammad Ali

Ali won the first 31 of his 61 professional fights, and in fact lost only five of them in all. Early in his career, he used to predict which round he would win in. He got the first 17 right!

I am the greatest. Not only do I knock ‘em out, I pick the round!

“FLOAT LIKE A BUTTERFLY” Muhammad Ali

Because of his long reach, Ali preferred head shots to body shots, and invented the “Ali Shuffle”, where he would raise himself and then shuffle his feet, appearing to dance, sometimes even throwing punches while shuffling.

Float like a butterfly.
Sting like a bee.
Your hands can’t hit
what your eyes can’t see.

"WE ALL HAVE DREAMS"
Jesse Owens

In 1936 the Olympic Games were held in Berlin, and Hitler wanted to use them to prove to the world that the "Aryan" people were the dominant race. To the German leader's obvious anger, Jesse Owens won four gold medals (for the 100 metres, 200 metres, 4 x 100-metre relay and long jump. He was (and still remains) an inspirational figure to millions.

We all have dreams. But in order to make dreams come into reality, it takes an awful lot of determination, dedication, self-discipline and effort.

"BLACK AMERICA WILL UNDERSTAND WHAT WE DID TONIGHT"
Tommie Smith

On October 17, 1968, at the height of the civil rights struggles in America, two black athletes – Tommie Smith and John Carlos – made a silent protest at the presentation ceremony for the 200 metres race, by raising their fists in the so-called "black power" salute during the playback of the US national anthem. They were subsequently suspended from the team, banned from the Olympic village and stripped of their medals. At a later press conference, Tommie Smith gave the following reason. (The silver medallist, white Australian Peter Norman, who wore a badge from the same anti-racist group was not disciplined).

If I win I am an American, not a black American. But if I did something bad then they would say "a Negro". We are black and we are proud of being black.

Black America will understand what we did tonight.

POLITICS

"IN THE NAME OF GOD, GO!"
Oliver Cromwell

The "Rump Parliament" was an interim body of a much reduced number of MPs ordered by Cromell to draft plans for new elections in a reformed English parliament. Despite being selected by Cromwell, the members disobeyed his orders and on April 20, 1653 he told the Members to leave. The full speech was censored after his death but reconstructed two centuries later by the historian Thomas Carlyle.

It is not fit that you should sit here any longer! You have been sat too long here for any good you have been doing lately. You shall now give place to better men!...You call yourselves a Parliament. You are no Parliament. I say you are no Parliament! Some of you are drunkards, some of you are living in open contempt of God's Commandments, following your own greedy appetites and the Devil's commandments. Corrupt unjust persons; scandalous to the profession of the Godpel; how can you be a Parliament for God's people? Depart, I say, and let us have done with you. In the name of God, go!

"I HAVE IN MY HAND A PIECE OF PAPER"
Joseph McCarthy

In the 1950s, many Americans were terrified of the possibility of Communist infiltration. Senator McCarthy was particularly zealous in rooting out anyone with what he saw as left-wing, and therefore anti-American and anti-Christian, leanings.

Today we are engaged in a final, all-out battle between Communistic atheism and Christianity. The modern champions of Communism have selected this as the time. And, ladies and gentlemen, the chips are down – they are truly down...

Can there be anyone here tonight who is so blind as to say that the war is not on? Can there be anyone who fails to realize that the Communist world has said, "The time is now" – that this is the time for the show-down between the democratic Christian world and the Communist atheistic world?

Unless we face this fact, we shall pay the price that must be paid by those who wait too long.

I have in my hand fifty-seven cases of individuals who would appear to be either card-carrying members or certainly loyal to the Communist Party, but who nevertheless are still helping to shape our foreign policy...

"HISTORY WILL ABSOLVE ME"
Fidel Castro

In July 1953 the young Cuban lawyer Fidel Castro led an armed revolt against the Moncada barracks. The revolt was unsuccessful. At his trial on October 16, which was held in secret, his speech from the dock was the inspiration for the subsequent Cuban revolution and concentrated on the justification for revolution against tyranny. The beginning and end sum up the spirit of the speech.

Honourable Judges, if there is in your hearts a vestige of love for your country, love for humanity, love for justice, listen carefully. I know that I will be silenced for many years; I know that there will be a conspiracy to bury me in oblivion. But my voice will not be stilled...

...I know that imprisonment will be harder for me than it has ever been for anyone, filled with cowardly threats and hideous cruelty. But I do not fear prison, as I do not fear the fury of the miserable tyrant who took the lives of seventy of my comrades. Condemn me. It does not matter. History will absolve me.

"CLEAR AND PRESENT DANGER"
John F. Kennedy

On October 22, 1962, President Kennedy made a television address to tell Americans about the build-up of Soviet weaponry on Cuba, including the installation of offensive nuclear missiles. After conferring with his advisers, Kennedy decided to blockade Cuba rather than attack the missile sites.

...This Government, as promised, has maintained the closest surveillance of the Soviet military build-up on the island of Cuba. Within the past week, unmistakable evidence has established the fact that a series of offensive missile sites is now in preparation on that imprisoned island. The purpose of these bases can be none other than to provide a nuclear strike capability against the Western Hemisphere...

The characteristics of these new missile sites indicate two distinct types of installations. Several of them include medium-range ballistic missiles capable of carrying a nuclear warhead for a distance of more than 1,000 nautical miles. Each of these missiles, in short, is capable of striking Washington DC, the Panama Canal, Cape Canaveral, Mexico City, or any other city in the southeastern part of the United States, in Central America, or in the Caribbean area.

This urgent transformation of Cuba into an important strategic base – by the presence of these large, long-range, and clearly offensive weapons of sudden mass destruction – constitutes an explicit threat to the peace and security of all the Americas, in flagrant and deliberate defiance of the Rio Pact of 1947, the traditions of this Nation and hemisphere, the joint resolution of the 87th Congress, the Charter of the United Nations, and my own public warnings to the Soviets on September 4 and 13. This action also contradicts the repeated assurances of Soviet spokesmen, both publicly and privately delivered, that the arms build-up in Cuba would retain its original defensive character, and that the Soviet Union had no need or desire to station strategic missiles on the territory of any other nation.

The size of this undertaking makes clear that it has been planned for some months. Yet only last month, after I had made clear the distinction between any introduction of ground-to-ground missiles and the existence of defensive anti-aircraft missiles, the Soviet Government publicly stated on September 11, and I quote, "the armaments and military equipment sent to Cuba are designed exclusively for defensive purposes," that, and I quote the Soviet Government, "there is no need for the Soviet Government to shift its weapons... for a retaliatory blow to any other country, for instance Cuba," and that, and I quote their government, "the Soviet Union has such powerful rockets to carry these nuclear warheads that there is no need to search for sites for them beyond the boundaries of the Soviet Union." That statement was false.

Only last Thursday, as evidence of this rapid offensive build-up was already in my hand, Soviet Foreign Minister Gromyko told me in my office that he was instructed to make it clear once again, as he said his government had already done, that Soviet assistance to Cuba, and I quote, "pursued solely the purpose of contributing to the defence capabilities of Cuba", that, and I quote him, "training by Soviet specialists of Cuban nationals in handling defensive armaments was by no means offensive, and if it were otherwise," Mr Gromyko went on, "the Soviet Government would never become involved in rendering such assistance." That statement also was false.

Neither the United States of America nor the world community of nations can tolerate deliberate deception and offensive threats on the part of any nation, large or small. We no longer live in a world where only the actual firing of weapons represents a sufficient challenge to a nation's security to constitute maximum peril. Nuclear weapons are so destructive and ballistic missiles are so swift, that any substantially increased possibility of their use or any sudden change in their deployment may well be regarded as a definite threat to peace.

For many years both the Soviet Union and the United States, recognizing this fact, have deployed strategic nuclear weapons with great care, never upsetting the precarious *status quo* which insured that these weapons would not be used in the absence of some vital challenge. Our own strategic missiles have never been transferred to the territory of any other nation under a cloak of secrecy and deception; and our history – unlike that of the Soviets since the end of World War II – demonstrates that we have no desire to dominate or conquer any other nation or impose our system upon its people...

In that sense, missiles in Cuba add to an already clear and present danger – although it should be noted the nations of Latin America have never previously been subjected to a potential nuclear threat...

Our policy has been one of patience and restraint, as befits a peaceful and powerful nation, which leads a worldwide alliance. We have been determined not to be diverted from our central concerns by mere irritants and fanatics. But now further action is required – and it is under way; and these actions may only be the beginning. We will not prematurely or unnecessarily risk the costs of worldwide nuclear war in which even the fruits of victory would be ashes in our mouth – but neither will we shrink from that risk at any time it must be faced...

But it is difficult to settle or even discuss these problems in an atmosphere of intimidation. That is why this latest Soviet threat – or any other threat which is made independently or in response to our actions this week – must and will be met with determination. Any hostile move anywhere in the world against the safety and freedom of peoples to whom we are committed – including in particular the brave people of West Berlin – will be met by whatever action is needed...

"GARIBALDI EXHORTS HIS GUERRILLAS TO FIGHT FOR A UNITED, INDEPENDENT ITALY"

Giuseppe Garibaldi

In the middle of the 19th century, Italy did not exist as a country, but as a collection of smaller states under the rule of Austria. In 1860, Giuseppe Garibaldi led his guerrilla army of 1,000 redshirts to victory in Sicily. By August they had entered Naples where he turned over his command to King Victor Emmanuel II. A year later, the sovereign kingdom of Italy was proclaimed, although Venice and Rome did not join for some years.

We must now consider the period which is just drawing to a close as almost the last stage of our national resurrection, and prepare ourselves to finish worthily the marvellous design of the elect of 20 generations, the completion of which Providence has reserved for this fortunate age.

Yes, young men, Italy owes to you an undertaking which has merited the applause of the universe. You have conquered and you will conquer still, because you are prepared for the tactics that decide the fate of battles. You are not unworthy of the men who entered the ranks of a Macedonian phalanx, and who contended not in vain with the proud conquerors of Asia. To this wonderful page in our country's history another more glorious still will be added, and the slave shall show at last to his free brothers a sharpened sword forged from the links of his fetters.

To arms, then, all of you! All of you! And the oppressors and the mighty shall disappear like dust. You, too, women, cast away all the cowards from your embraces; they will give you only cowards for children, and you who are the daughters of the land of beauty must bear children who are noble and brave. Let timid doctrinaires depart from among us to carry their servility and their miserable fears elsewhere. This people is its own master. It wishes to be the brother of other peoples, but to look on the insolent with a proud glance, not to grovel before them imploring its own freedom. It will no longer follow in the trail of men whose hearts are foul. No! No! No!

Providence has presented Italy with Victor Emmanuel. Every Italian should rally round him. By the side of Victor Emmanuel every quarrel should be forgotten, all rancor depart. Once more I repeat my battle-cry: "To arms, all – all of you!" If March 1861 does not find one million Italians in arms, then alas for liberty, alas for the life of Italy. Ah, no, far be from me a thought which I loathe like poison. March of 1861, or if need be February, will find us all at our post-Italians of Calatafimi, Palermo, Ancona, the Volturno, Castelfidardo and Isernia, and with us every man of this land who is not a coward or a slave. Let all of us rally round the glorious hero of Palestro and give the last blow to the crumbling edifice of tyranny. Receive, then, my gallant young volunteers, at the honoured conclusion of ten battles, one word of farewell from me.

I utter this word with deepest affection and from the very bottom of my heart. Today I am obliged to retire, but for a few days only. The hour of battle will find me with you again, by the side of the champions of Italian liberty. Let those only return to their homes who are called by the imperative duties which they owe to their families, and those who by their glorious wounds have deserved the credit of their country. These, indeed, will serve Italy in their homes by their counsel, by the very aspect of the scars which adorn their youthful brows. Apart from these, let all others remain to guard our glorious banners. We shall meet again before long to march together to the redemption of our brothers who are still slaves of the stranger. We shall meet again before long to march to new triumphs.

"SENATOR, YOU ARE NO JACK KENNEDY"
Lloyd Bentsen

On October 5, 1988 US Vice-Presidential candidates Senator Lloyd Bentsen and Senator Dan Quayle met in a televised debate. During the campaign Quayle had more than once reacted to accusations of lack of political experience with the comment that he had as much political experience as John F. Kennedy. Bentsen's rejoinder did not stop Bush and Quayle winning the election, but was the start of the decline in the latter's reputation.

Quayle: "...I have as much experience in the Congress as Jack Kennedy did when he sought the presidency. I will be prepared to deal with the people in the Bush administration, if that unfortunate event would ever occur."

Bentsen: "Senator, I served with Jack Kennedy, I knew Jack Kennedy, Jack Kennedy was a friend of mine. Senator, you are no Jack Kennedy."

"THE ARMY WILL NOT GO AGAINST THE PEOPLE"
Boris Yeltsin

On August 20, 1991 President Mikhail Gorbachev was due to sign a new treaty of union to preserve what was left of the USSR under a more liberal regime, but two days before he was detained at his summer residence by hardline Communist plotters who tried to seize power. The Russian president, Boris Yeltsin, rushed to the White House in Moscow. Thousands of citizens arrived to defend the building from the surrounding troops. A tank unit and a division of paratroopers switched sides and Yeltsin climbed on to the tank to denounce the plotters. The speech is memorable chiefly for the circumstances. The troops were never ordered to attack the White House, and the following day most of the *coup* leaders fled.

The reactionaries will not achieve their goals; the army will not go against the people.

"TOMORROW YOU MAY HAVE ANOTHER PRESIDENT"
Mikhail Gorbachev

After the attempted *coup* by hardline communists in August 1991– and particularly the public reaction to it – Soviet president Gorbachev realized that the process of liberalization had to be speeded up. On September 3 he addressed the Congress of People's Deputies, concluding:

... If there have been mistakes, if there have been miscalculations in tactics and in measures – but he [Gorbachev himself] also did not notice that it was necessary to move more rapidly along the path of liberating ourselves from those totalitarian structures... Today you have a president. Tomorrow you may have another president. In any case, we are all one, side by side, and we shouldn't spit on each other.

“A CONTAMINATED MORAL ENVIRONMENT”
Vaclav Havel

On January 1, 1990 Vaclav Havel, the playwright and freely elected president of Czechoslovakia, made a speech to the nation, detailing what he saw as the moral and economic issues it faced.

My dear fellow citizens, for forty years you heard from my predecessors on this day different variations of the same theme: how our country flourished, how many million tons of steel we produced, how happy we all were...

I assume you did not propose me for this office so that I, too, would lie to you...Our country is not flourishing...

But all this is still not the main problem. The worst thing is that we live in a contaminated moral environment. We fell morally ill because we became used to saying something different from what we thought. We learned not to believe in anything, to ignore each other, to care only about ourselves...

If we realize this, then all the horrors that the new Czechosovak democracy inherited will cease to appear so terrible. If we realize this, hope will return to our hearts...

"THE THREEFOLD YOKE OF IGNORANCE, TYRANNY AND VICE"
Simón Bolívar

Simón Bolívar headed the political and military struggle for South America's independence from Spain, leading the revolutions that resulted in the freedom of the countries now known as Bolivia, Colombia, Ecuador, Panama and Peru. He made the following address to the opening of the Second National Congress of Venezuela on Feburary 15, 1819.

In absolute systems, the central power is unlimited. The will of the despot is the supreme law, arbitrarily enforced by subordinates who take part in the organized oppression in proportion to the authority that they wield. They are charged with civil, political, military and religious functions; but, in the final analysis, the satraps of Persia are Persian, the pashas of the Grand Turk are Turks, and the sultans of Tartary are Tartars. China does not seek her mandarins in the homeland of Genghis Khan, her conqueror. America, on the contrary, received everything from Spain, who, in effect, deprived her of the experience that she would have gained from the exercise of an active tyranny by not allowing her to take part in her own domestic affairs and administration. This exclusion made it impossible for us to acquaint ourselves with the management of public affairs; nor did we enjoy that personal consideration, of such great value in major revolutions, that the brilliance of power inspires in the eyes of the multitude. In brief, gentlemen, we were deliberately kept in ignorance and cut off from the world in all matters relating to the science of government.

Subject to the threefold yoke of ignorance, tyranny and vice, the American people have been unable to acquire knowledge, power or [civic] virtue. The lessons we received and the models we studied, as pupils of such pernicious teachers, were most destructive. We have been ruled more by deceit than by force, and we have been degraded more by vice than by superstition. Slavery is the daughter of darkness: an ignorant people is a blind instrument of its own destruction. Ambition and intrigue abuse the credulity and experience of men lacking all political, economic, and civic knowledge; they adopt pure illusion as reality; they take licence for liberty, treachery for patriotism and vengeance for justice. This situation is similar to that of the robust blind man who, beguiled by his strength, strides forward with all the assurance of one who can see, but, upon hitting every variety of obstacle, finds himself unable to retrace his steps.

If a people, perverted by their training, succeed in achieving their liberty, they will soon lose it, for it would be of no avail to endeavour to explain to them that happiness consists in the practice of virtue; that the rule of law is more powerful than the rule of tyrants, because, as the laws are more inflexible, everyone should submit to their beneficent austerity; that proper morals, and not force, are the bases of law; and that to practise justice is to practise liberty. Therefore, legislators, your work is so much the more arduous, inasmuch as you have to re-educate men who have been corrupted by erroneous illusions and false incentives. Liberty, says Rousseau, is a succulent morsel, but one difficult to digest. Our weak fellow-citizens will have to strengthen their spirit greatly before they can digest the wholesome nutriment of freedom. Their limbs benumbed by chains, their sight dimmed by the darkness of dungeons, and their strength sapped by the pestilence of servitude, are they capable of marching toward the august temple of Liberty without faltering? Can they come near enough to bask in its brilliant rays and to breathe freely the pure air which reigns therein?...

WAR

"THE WAR TO END WARS"
Woodrow Wilson

After World War I, many Americans felt that American participation in the conflict in Europe had been to no purpose and that their sacrifices, particularly those of thousands of young Americans who died, had been in vain. President Wilson believed passionately that the League of Nations was the only way to prevent another bloody conflict.

I want to remind you how the permanency of peace is at the heart of this treaty. This is not merely a treaty of peace with Germany...it is nothing less than world settlement, and at the centre of that stands the covenant for the future we call the Covenant of the League of Nations. Without it the treaty cannot be worked and without it it is a mere temporary arrangement with Germany. The covenant of the League of Nations is the instrumentality (means) for the maintenance of peace.

If the treaty is not ratified by the Senate, the war will have been fought in vain, and the world will be thrown into chaos. I promised our soldiers, when I asked them to take up arms, that it was a war to end wars...

"MY PATIENCE IS AT AN END"
Adolf Hitler

While negotiating the Munich Agreement, Hitler made a speech in Berlin on September 26, 1938, claiming that if Czechoslovakia ceded the Sudetenland, Germany would stop claiming territory.

...The history of the problem is as follows: in 1918 under the watchword "The Right of the Peoples to Self-determination" Central Europe was torn in pieces and was newly formed by certain crazy so-called "statesmen". Without regard for the origin of the peoples, without regard for either their wish as nations or for economic necessities, Central Europe at that time was broken up into atoms and new so-called states were arbitrarily formed. To this procedure Czechoslovakia owes its existence. This Czech state began with a single lie and the father of this lie was named Beneš. This Mr Beneš at that time appeared in Versailles and he first of all gave the assurance that there was a Czechoslovak nation. He was forced to invent this lie in order to give the slender number of his own fellow-countrymen a somewhat greater range and thus a fuller justification...

So in the end through Mr Beneš these Czechs annexed Slovakia. Since this state did not seem fitted to live, out of hand three and a half million Germans were taken in violation of their right to self-determination and their wish for self-determination...

That is this state which then later proceeded to call itself Czechoslovakia – in violation of the right of the peoples to self-determination, in violation of the clear wish and will of the nations to which this violence had been done...

Mr Beneš now places his hopes on the world! And he and his diplomats make no secret of the fact. They state: it is our hope that

Chamberlain will be overthrown, that Daladier will be removed, that on every hand revolutions are on the way. They place their hope on Soviet Russia. He still thinks then that he will be able to evade the fulfilment of his obligationns.

And then I can say only one thing: now two men stand arrayed one against the other: there is Mr Beneš and here stand I. We are two men of a different make-up. In the great struggle of the peoples while Mr Beneš was sneaking about through the world, I as a decent German soldier did my duty. And now today I stand over against this man as the soldier of my people!

But in the same way I desire to state before the German people that with regard to the problem of the Sudeten Germans my patience is now at an end! I have made Mr Beneš an offer which is nothing but the carrying into effect of what he himself has promised. The decision now lies in his hands: Peace or War...

In this hour we all wish to form a common will and that will must be stronger than every hardship and every danger.

And if this will is stronger than hardship and danger then one day it will break down hardship and danger.

We are determined!

Now let Mr Beneš make his choice!

“PEACE FOR OUR TIME”
Neville Chamberlain

Just four days after Hitler’s ominous warning at the Berlin Sportspalast in 1938, British Prime Minister Neville Chamberlain returned to London, firmly believing that conceding large areas of Czechoslovakia to Germany had laid to rest Hitler’s territorial ambitions. He made the following impromptu speech from a first-floor window of 10 Downing Street.

My good friends, this is the second time in our history that there has come back from Germany to Downing Street peace with honour...I believe it is peace for our time. We thank you from the bottom of our hearts...And now I recommend you to go home and sleep quietly in your beds.

"THIS COUNTRY IS AT WAR WITH GERMANY"
Neville Chamberlain

Less than a year after signing the Munich Agreement, Hitler ordered his troops into Poland. Chamberlain made the following radio address on September 3, 1939.

I am speaking to you from the Cabinet Room at 10 Downing Street.

This morning the British Ambassador in Berlin handed the German Government a final Note stating that, unless we heard from them by 11 o'clock that they were prepared at once to withdraw their troops from Poland, a state of war would exist between us.

I have to tell you now that no such undertaking has been received, and that consequently this country is at war with Germany.

You can imagine what a bitter blow it is to me that all my long struggle to win peace has failed. Yet I cannot believe that there is anything more or anything different that I could have done and that would have been more successful.

Up to the very last it would have been quite possible to have arranged a peaceful and honourable settlement between Germany and Poland, but Hitler would not have it. He had evidently made up his mind to attack Poland whatever happened, and although he now says he put forward reasonable proposals which were rejected by the Poles, that is not a true statement.

The proposals were never shown to the Poles, nor to us, and, though they were announced in a German broadcast on Thursday night, Hitler did not wait to hear comments on them, but ordered his troops to cross the Polish frontier. His action shows convincingly that there is no chance of expecting that this man will ever give up his practice of using force to gain his will. He can only be stopped by force.

We and France are today, in fulfilment of our obligations, going to the aid of Poland, who is so bravely resisting this wicked and unprovoked attack on her people. We have a clear conscience. We have done all that any country could do to establish peace. The situation in which no word given by Germany's ruler could be trusted and no people or country could feel themselves safe has become intolerable. And now that we have resolved to finish it, I know that you will all play your part with calmness and courage.

At such a moment as this the assurances of support that we have received from the Empire are a source of profound encouragement to us.

When I have finished speaking certain detailed announcements will be made on behalf of the Government. Give these your closest attention. The Government have made plans under which it will be possible to carry on the work of the nation in the days of stress and strain that may be ahead. But these plans need your help.

You may be taking your part in the fighting services or as a volunteer in one of the branches of Civil Defence. If so you will report for duty in accordance with the instructions you have received. You may be engaged in work essential to the prosecution of war for the maintenance of the life of the people – in factories, in transport, in public utility concerns, or in the supply of other necessaries of life. If so, it is of vital importance that you should carry on with your jobs.

Now may God bless you all. May He defend the right. It is the evil things that we shall be fighting against – brute force, bad faith, injustice, oppression and persecution – and against them I am certain that the right will prevail.

"BLOOD, TOIL, TEARS AND SWEAT"
Winston Churchill

Only a few days after taking over as Prime Minister, Churchill entered the House of Commons on May 13, 1940 to make a brief speech about forming an administration consisting of members from all of the major parties. He concluded:

I say to the House as I said to ministers who have joined this government, I have nothing to offer but blood, toil, tears and sweat. We have before us an ordeal of the most grievous kind. We have before us many, many months of struggle and suffering.

You ask, what is our policy? I say it is to wage war by land, sea and air. War with all our might and with all the strength God has given us, and to wage war against a monstrous tyranny never surpassed in the dark and lamentable catalogue of human crime. That is our policy.

You ask, what is our aim? I can answer in one word. It is victory. Victory at all costs; victory in spite of all terrors; victory, however long and hard the road may be, for without victory there is no survival.

I take up my task in buoyancy and hope. I feel sure that our cause will not be suffered to fail among men. I feel entitled at this juncture, at this time, to claim the aid of all and to say, "Come then, let us go forward together with our united strength."

"WE SHALL FIGHT THEM ON THE BEACHES"
Winston Churchill

After the allied defeat and ensuing rescue of more than 335,000 men from the beaches around Dunkirk on the north coast of France in late May and early June 1940, Winston Churchill made a radio broadcast on June 4, urging the British people to fight on.

Even though large tracts of Europe and many old and famous states have fallen or may fall into the grip of the Gestapo and all the odious apparatus of Nazi rule, we shall not flag or fail.

We shall go on to the end, we shall fight in France, we shall fight on the seas and oceans, we shall fight with growing confidence and growing strength in the air, we shall defend our Island, whatever the cost may be, we shall fight on the beaches, we shall fight on the landing grounds, we shall fight in the fields and in the streets, we shall fight in the hills; we shall never surrender, and even if, which I do not for a moment believe, this Island or a large part of it were subjugated and starving, then our Empire beyond the seas, armed and guarded by the British Fleet, would carry on the struggle, until, in God's good time, the New World, with all its power and might, steps forth to the rescue and the liberation of the old.

“SCORCHED EARTH”
Joseph Stalin

On June 22, 1941, German troops crossed the poorly defended Soviet borders, despite the two countries’ non-aggression pact, signed in 1939. On July 3, Stalin broadcast the following speech, urging the population both to fight and to destroy anything that the invading armies might use. Like many leaders before him, he also called for third columnists to be weeded out and denounced.

Comrades! Citizens! Brothers and sisters! Men of our army and navy! I am addressing you, my friends.

The perfidious military attack on our fatherland, begun on June 22 by Hitler’s Germany, is continuing...

A grave danger hangs over our country...

Above all, it is essential that our people, the Soviet people, should understand the full immensity of the danger that threatens our country and abandon all complacency, all heedlessness, all those moods of peaceful, constructive work which were so natural before the war but which are fatal today, when war has fundamentally changed everything...

...there must be no room in our ranks for whimperers and cowards, for panicmongers and deserters; our people must know no fear in the fight and must selflessly join our patriotic war of liberation, or war against the Fascist enslavers...

The peoples of the Soviet Union must rise against the enemy and defend their rights and their land. The Red Army, Red Navy and all citizens of the Soviet Union must defend every inch of Soviet soil, must fight to the last drop of blood for our towns and villages, must display the daring initiative and intelligence that are inherent in our people.

We must wage a ruthless fight against all disorganizers of the rear, deserters, panicmongers, rumourmongers, exterminate spies, diversionists, enemy parachutists, rendering rapid aid in all this to our destroyer battalions. We must bear in mind that the enemy is crafty, unscrupulous, experienced in deception and dissemination of false rumours.

We must reckon with all this and not fall victim to provocation. All who by their panicmongering and cowardice hinder the work of defence, no matter who they are, must be immediately hauled before a military tribunal...

Collective farmers must drive off all their cattle and turn over their grain to the state authorities for transportation to the rear. All valuable property including non-ferrous metals, grain and fuel which cannot be withdrawn must without fail be destroyed.

In areas occupied by the enemy, guerrilla units, mounted and on foot, must be formed; diversionist groups must be organized to combat enemy troops, to foment guerrilla warfare everywhere, to blow up bridges, roads, damage telephone and telegraph lines, and to set fire to forests, stores and transports...

All our forces for the support of our heroic Red Army and our glorious Red Navy!

All the forces of the people – for the demolition of the enemy!

Forward, to our victory!

"WHAT CONSTITUTES AN AMERICAN?"
Harold Ickes

As had happened with World War I, America held off from direct military involvement at the beginning of World War II, although the government was supplying food aid. Because of anti-Communist fears and pro-Fascist propaganda, many Americans were coming around to the idea that it would be wrong to intervene in events on the other side of the Atlantic Ocean. Secretary of the Interior Harold Ickes, in this speech given on May 18, 1941, issued a call to the American people to remember the ideals with which their country had been founded and also a bleak warning of the future if America buried its collective head in the sand and Germany's expansionism was unchecked. America joined in the war a little under six months later after the Japanese attack on Pearl Harbor.

...What has happened to our vaunted idealism? Why have some of us been behaving like scared chickens? Where is the million-throated, democratic voice of America?...

For years it has been dinned into us that we are a weak nation; that we are an inefficient people; that we are simple-minded. For years we have been told that we are beaten, decayed, and that no part of the world belongs to us any longer.

I say that it is time for the great American people to raise its voice and cry out in mighty triumph what it is to be an American. And why it is that only Americans, with the aid of our brave allies – yes, let's call them "allies" – the British, can and will build the only future worth having. I mean a future, not of concentration camps, not of physical torture and mental straitjackets, not of sawdust bread or of sawdust Caesars – I mean a future when free men will live free lives in dignity and in security...

What constitutes an American? Not colour nor race nor religion. Not the pedigree of his family nor the place of his birth. Not the coincidence of his citizenship. Not his social status nor his bank account. Not his trade nor his profession. An American is one who loves justice and believes in the dignity of man. An American is one who will fight for his freedom and that of his neighbour. An American is one who will sacrifice property, ease and security in order that he and his children may retain the rights of free men. An American is one in whose heart is engraved the immortal second sentence of the Declaration of Independence...

We Americans know that freedom, like peace, is indivisible. We cannot retain our liberty if three-fourths of the world is enslaved. Brutality, injustice and slavery, if practised as dictators would have them, universally and systematically, in the long run would destroy us as surely as a fire raging in our nearby neighbour's house would burn ours if we didn't help to put out his.

If we are to retain our own freedom, we must do everything within our power to aid Britain. We must also do everything to restore to the conquered peoples their freedom. This means the Germans too...

This is why the British are not fighting for themselves alone. They are fighting to preserve freedom for mankind. For the moment, the battleground is the British Isles. But they are fighting our war; they are the first soldiers in trenches that are also our front-line trenches...

These hundreds of millions of liberty-loving people, now oppressed, constitute the greatest sixth column in history. They have the will to destroy the Nazi gangsters...

The fight for Britain is in its crucial stages. We must give the British everything we have. And by everything, I mean everything needed to beat the life out of our common enemy...

"A DAY THAT WILL LIVE IN INFAMY"
Franklin D. Roosevelt

On December 7, 1941, Japanese fighter planes attacked Pearl Harbor, Hawaii, and other US bases around the Pacific Ocean. The following day, President Roosevelt appeared before the US Congress asking for a declaration of war.

Mr. Vice President, Mr. Speaker, members of the Senate and the House of Representatives:

Yesterday, December 7, 1941 – a date that will live in infamy – the United States of America was suddenly and deliberately attacked by naval and air forces of the Empire of Japan.

The United States was at peace with that nation, and, at the solicitation of Japan, was still in conversation with its government and its Emperor looking toward the maintenance of peace in the Pacific.

Indeed, one hour after Japanese air squadrons had commenced bombing in the American island of Oahu, the Japanese Ambassador to the United States and his colleague delivered to our Secretary of State a formal reply to a recent American message. And, while this reply stated that it seemed useless to continue the existing diplomatic negotiations, it contained no threat or hint of war or of armed attack.

It will be recorded that the distance of Hawaii from Japan makes it obvious that the attack was deliberately planned many days or even weeks ago. During the intervening time the Japanese Government has deliberately sought to deceive the United States by false statements and expressions of hope for continued peace.

The attack yesterday on the Hawaiian Islands has caused severe damage to American naval and military forces. I regret to tell you that very many American lives have been lost. In addition, American ships have been reported torpedoed on the high seas between San Francisco and Honolulu.

Yesterday the Japanese Government also launched an attack against Malaya.
Last night Japanese forces attacked Hong Kong.
Last night Japanese forces attacked Guam.
Last night Japanese forces attacked the Philippine Islands.
Last night the Japanese attacked Wake Island.
And this morning the Japanese attacked Midway Island.

Japan has therefore undertaken a surprise offensive extending throughout the Pacific area. The facts of yesterday and today speak for themselves. The people of the United States have already formed their opinions and well understand the implications to the very life and safety of our nation.

As Commander-in-Chief of the Army and Navy I have directed that all measures be taken for our defence, that always will our whole nation remember the character of the onslaught against us.

No matter how long it may take us to overcome this premeditated invasion, the American people, in their righteous might, will win through to absolute victory.

I believe that I interpret the will of the Congress and of the people when I assert that we will not only defend ourselves to the uttermost but will make it very certain that this form of treachery shall never again endanger us.

Hostilities exist. There is no blinking at the fact that our people, our territory and our interests are in grave danger.

With confidence in our armed forces, with the unbounding determination of our people, we will gain the inevitable triumph.

So help us God.

I ask that the Congress declare that since the unprovoked and dastardly attack by Japan on Sunday, December 7, 1941, a state of war has existed between the United States and the Japanese Empire.

"THE DEATH OF ONE MAN IS A TRAGEDY"
Joseph Stalin

Stalin's comment made to Churchill at the Potsdam conference in 1945 now seems bitterly ironic, given how many millions of people died, were dispossessed or imprisoned during his 30 years in power.

The death of one man is a tragedy. The death of millions is a statistic.

"SIXTEEN HOURS AGO"
Harry S. Truman

On August 6, 1945, the following statement was released to the press on behalf of President Truman, in which he announced that an atomic bomb had been dropped on Hiroshima and that the Japanese government should surrender as soon as possible to avoid further action; he also detailed America's plans for military and civilian use of atomic science. Because the Japanese government made no immediate response, a second bomb was dropped on Nagasaki three days later. A week after that, the Japanese government surrendered. It is still argued whether Truman did, in fact, know that Hiroshima was a city.

Sixteen hours ago an American airplane dropped one bomb on Hiroshima, an important Japanese army base. That bomb had more power than 20,000 tons of TNT. It had more than 2,000 times the blast power of the British "Grand Slam", which is the largest bomb ever yet used in the history of warfare.

The Japanese began the war from the air at Pearl Harbor. They have been repaid many fold. And the end is not yet. With this bomb we have now added a new and revolutionary increase in destruction to supplement the growing power of our armed forces. In their present form these bombs are now in production, and even more powerful forms are in development.

It is an atomic bomb. It is a harnessing of the basic power of the universe. The force from which the sun draws its power has been loosed against those who brought war to the Far East.

Before 1939, it was the accepted belief of scientists that it was theoretically possible to release atomic energy. But no one knew any practical method of doing it. By 1942, however, we knew that the Germans were working feverishly to find a way to add atomic energy to the other engines of war with which they hoped to enslave the world. But they failed. We may be grateful to Providence that the Germans got the V-ls and V-2s late and in limited quantities and even more grateful that they did not get the atomic bomb at all.

The battle of the laboratories held fateful risks for us as well as the battles of the air, land and sea, and we have now won the battle of the laboratories as we have won the other battles.

Beginning in 1940, before Pearl Harbor, scientific knowledge useful in war was pooled between the United States and Great Britain, and many priceless helps to our victories have come from that arrangement. Under that general policy the research on the atomic bomb was begun. With American and British scientists working together we entered the race of discovery against the Germans.

The United States had available the large number of scientists of distinction in the many needed areas of knowledge. It had the tremendous industrial and financial resources necessary for the project, and they could be devoted to it without undue impairment of other vital war work. In the United States the laboratory work and the production plants, on which a substantial start had already been made, would be out of reach of enemy bombing, while at that time Britain was exposed to constant air attack and was still threatened with the possibility of invasion. For these reasons Prime Minister Churchill and President Roosevelt agreed that it was wise to carry on the project here.

We now have two great plants and many lesser works devoted to the production of atomic power. Employment during peak construction numbered 125,000 and over 65,000 individuals are even now engaged in operating the plants. Many have worked there for two and a half years. Few know what they have been producing. They see great quantities of material going in and they see nothing coming out of these plants, for the physical size of the explosive charge is exceedingly small. We have spent $2,000,000 on the greatest scientific gamble in history – and won.

But the greatest marvel is not the size of the enterprise, its secrecy, nor its cost, but the achievement of scientific brains in putting together infinitely complex pieces of knowledge held by many men in different fields of science into a workable plan. And hardly less marvelous has been the capacity of industry to design, and of labour to operate, the machines and methods to do things never done before so that the brainchild of many minds came forth in physical shape and performed as it was supposed to do. Both science and industry worked under the direction of the United States army, which achieved a unique success in managing so diverse a problem in the advancement of knowledge in an amazingly short time. It is doubtful if such another combination could be got together in the world. What has been done is the greatest achievement of organized science in history. It was done under high pressure and without failure.

We are now prepared to obliterate more rapidly and completely every productive enterprise the Japanese have above ground in any city. We shall destroy their docks, their factories, and their communications. Let there be no mistake; we shall completely destroy Japan's power to make war.

It was to spare the Japanese people from utter destruction that the ultimatum of July 26 was issued at Potsdam. Their leaders promptly rejected that ultimatum. If they do not now accept our terms they may expect a rain of ruin from the air, the like of which has never been seen on this earth. Behind this air attack will follow sea and land forces in such numbers and power as they have not yet seen and with the fighting skill of which they are already well aware.

The secretary of war, who has kept in personal touch with all phases of the project, will immediately make public a statement giving further details.

His statement will give facts concerning the sites at Oak Ridge near Knoxville, Tennessee, and at Richland near Pasco, Washington, and an installation near Santa Fe, New Mexico. Although the workers at the sites have been making materials to be used in producing the greatest destructive force in history, they have not themselves been in danger beyond that of many other occupations, for the utmost care has been taken of their safety.

The fact that we can release atomic energy ushers in a new era in man's understanding of nature's forces. Atomic energy may in the future supplement the power that now comes from coal, oil and falling water, but at present it cannot be produced on a basis to compete with them commercially. Before that comes there must be a long period of intensive research.

It has never been the habit of the scientists of this country or the policy of this government to withhold from the world scientific knowledge. Normally, therefore, everything about the work with atomic energy would be made public.

But under present circumstances it is not intended to divulge the technical processes of production or all the military applications, pending further examination of possible methods of protecting us and the rest of the world from the danger of sudden destruction.

I shall recommend that the Congress of the United States consider promptly the establishment of an appropriate commission to control the production and use of atomic power within the United States. I shall give further consideration and make further recommendations to the Congress as to how atomic power can become a powerful and forceful influence towards the maintenance of world peace.

"AN IRON CURTAIN"
Winston Churchill

Less than a year after the end of World War II, Churchill made the speech from which these extracts are taken, outlining his views of the expansion of Soviet control in Eastern Europe and how he thought it could best be dealt with in order to avoid a third, devastating war.

...I have a strong admiration and regard for the valiant Russian people and for my wartime comrade, Marshal Stalin. There is deep sympathy and goodwill in Britain – and I doubt not here also – toward the peoples of all the Russias and a resolve to persevere through many differences and rebuffs in establishing lasting friendships.

It is my duty, however, to place before you certain facts about the present position in Europe...

From Stettin in the Baltic to Trieste in the Adriatic an iron curtain has descended across the Continent. Behind that line lie all the capitals of the ancient states of Central and Eastern Europe...

The safety of the world, ladies and gentlemen, requires a unity in Europe, from which no nation should be permanently outcast. It is from the quarrels of the strong parent races in Europe that the world wars we have witnessed, or which occurred in former times, have sprung...

From what I have seen of our Russian friends and allies during the war, I am convinced that there is nothing they admire so much as strength, and there is nothing for which they have less respect than for weakness, especially military weakness.

For that reason the old doctrine of a balance of power is unsound. We cannot afford, if we can help it, to work on narrow margins, offering temptations to a trial of strength...

We must not let it happen again. This can only be achieved by reaching now, in 1946, a good understanding on all points with Russia under the general authority of the United Nations Organization and by the maintenance of that good understanding through many peaceful years, by the whole strength of the English-speaking world and all its connections.

"NUCLEAR WARFARE"
Albert Einstein

After America bombed Hiroshima and Nagasaki, Einstein was horrified by the military uses that his work had – unintentionally – contributed to and vehemently against the idea of a nuclear deterrent.

The release of atom power has changed everything except our way of thinking...the solution to this problem lies in the heart of mankind. If only I had known, I should have become a watchmaker.

"THE WAR ON TERROR"
George W. Bush

On September 20, 2001, President George W. Bush addressed a joint session of Congress. The following extracts are the first indication of the American government's response to the terrorist strikes.

Tonight, we are a country awakened to danger and called to defend freedom. Our grief has turned to anger and anger to resolution. Whether we bring our enemies to justice or bring justice to our enemies, justice will be done...

On September the 11th, enemies of freedom committed an act of war against our country. Americans have known wars, but for the past 136 years they have been wars on foreign soil, except for one Sunday in 1941. Americans have known the casualties of war, but not at the centre of a great city on a peaceful morning...

Americans have many questions tonight. Americans are asking, "Who attacked our country?"

The evidence we have gathered all points to a collection of loosely affiliated terrorist organizations known as al-Qaida. They are some of the murderers indicted for bombing American embassies in Tanzania and Kenya and responsible for bombing the USS *Cole*.

The terrorists practise a fringe form of Islamic extremism that has been rejected by Muslim scholars and the vast majority of Muslim clerics; a fringe movement that perverts the peaceful teachings of Islam.

The terrorists' directive commands them to kill Christians and Jews, to kill all Americans and make no distinctions among

military and civilians, including women and children.
This group and its leader, a person named Osama bin Laden, are linked to many other organizations in different countries, including the Egyptian Islamic Jihad, the Islamic Movement of Uzbekistan...

The leadership of al-Qaida has great influence in Afghanistan and supports the Taliban regime in controlling most of that country. In Afghanistan we see al-Qaida's vision for the world. Afghanistan's people have been brutalized, many are starving and many have fled...

The United States respects the people of Afghanistan – after all, we are currently its largest source of humanitarian aid – but we condemn the Taliban regime.

It is not only repressing its own people, it is threatening people everywhere by sponsoring and sheltering and supplying terrorists.

By aiding and abetting murder, the Taliban regime is committing murder. And tonight the United States of America makes the following demands on the Taliban.

Deliver to United States authorities all of the leaders of al-Qaida who hide in your land.

Release all foreign nationals, including American citizens you have unjustly imprisoned. Protect foreign journalists, diplomats and aid workers in your country. Close immediately and permanently every terrorist training camp in Afghanistan. And hand over every terrorist and every person and their support structure to appropriate authorities.

Give the United States full access to terrorist training camps, so we can make sure they are no longer operating.

These demands are not open to negotiation or discussion.

The Taliban must act and act immediately.
They will hand over the terrorists, or they will share in their fate...

The terrorists are traitors to their own faith, trying, in effect, to hijack Islam itself.

The enemy of America is not our many Muslim friends. It is not our many Arab friends. Our enemy is a radical network of terrorists and every government that supports them.

Our war on terror begins with al-Qaida, but it does not end there.

It will not end until every terrorist group of global reach has been found, stopped and defeated.

Americans are asking, "Why do they hate us?"

They hate what they see right here in this chamber: a democratically elected government. Their leaders are self-appointed. They hate our freedoms: our freedom of religion, our freedom of speech, our freedom to vote and assemble and disagree with each other...

Now this war will not be like the war against Iraq a decade ago, with a decisive liberation of territory and a swift conclusion. It will not look like the air war above Kosovo two years ago, where no ground troops were used and not a single American was lost in combat.

Our response involves far more than instant retaliation and isolated strikes. Americans should not expect one battle, but a lengthy campaign unlike any other we have ever seen. It may include dramatic strikes visible on TV and covert operations secret even in success.

We will starve terrorists of funding, turn them one against another, drive them from place to place until there is no refuge or no rest.

And we will pursue nations that provide aid or safe haven to terrorism. Every nation in every region now has a decision to make: either you are with us, or you are with the terrorists.

From this day forward, any nation that continues to harbour or support terrorism will be regarded by the United States as a hostile regime. Our nation has been put on notice, we're not immune from attack. We will take defensive measures against terrorism to protect Americans...

The hour is coming when America will act, and you will make us proud.

This is not, however, just America's fight. And what is at stake is not just America's freedom.

This is the world's fight. This is civilization's fight. This is the fight of all who believe in progress and pluralism, tolerance and freedom.

We ask every nation to join us...

We're in a fight for our principles, and our first responsibility is to live by them. No one should be singled out for unfair treatment or unkind words because of their ethnic background or religious faith....

As long as the United States of America is determined and strong, this will not be an age of terror. This will be an age of liberty here and across the world...

Our nation, this generation, will lift the dark threat of violence from our people and our future. We will rally the world to this cause by our efforts, by our courage. We will not tire, we will not falter and we will not fail...

“AXIS OF EVIL”
George W. Bush

The State of the Union address on January 29, 2002 continued the theme of President Bush’s September 20 address to Congress. The “axis of evil” tag is reminiscent of Reagan’s evil empire.

We last met in an hour of shock and suffering. In four short months, our nation has comforted the victims, begun to rebuild New York and the Pentagon, rallied a great coalition, captured, arrested, and rid the world of thousands of terrorists, destroyed Afghanistan's terrorist training camps, saved a people from starvation, and freed a country from brutal oppression.

The American flag flies again over our embassy in Kabul. Terrorists who once occupied Afghanistan now occupy cells at Guantanamo Bay. And terrorist leaders who urged followers to sacrifice their lives are running for their own...

The men and women of our armed forces have delivered a message now clear to every enemy of the United States: even 7,000 miles away, across oceans and continents, on mountaintops and in caves – you will not escape the justice of this nation...

What we have found in Afghanistan confirms that, far from ending there, our war against terror is only beginning. Most of the 19 men who hijacked planes on September the 11th were trained in Afghanistan's camps, and so were tens of thousands of others. Thousands of dangerous killers, schooled in the methods of murder, often supported by outlaw regimes, are now spread throughout the world like ticking time bombs, set to go off without warning...
Our nation will continue to be steadfast and patient and persistent in the pursuit of two great objectives. First, we will shut down terrorist camps, disrupt terrorist plans and bring terrorists to

justice. And, second, we must prevent the terrorists and regimes who seek chemical, biological or nuclear weapons from threatening the United States and the world...

But some governments will be timid in the face of terror. And make no mistake about it: if they do not act, America will...

Our second goal is to prevent regimes that sponsor terror from threatening America or our friends and allies with weapons of mass destruction. Some of these regimes have been pretty quiet since September the 11th. But we know their true nature. North Korea is a regime arming with missiles and weapons of mass destruction, while starving its citizens.

Iran aggressively pursues these weapons and exports terror, while an unelected few repress the Iranian people's hope for freedom.

Iraq continues to flaunt its hostility toward America and to support terror. The Iraqi regime has plotted to develop anthrax, and nerve gas, and nuclear weapons for over a decade. This is a regime that has already used poison gas to murder thousands of its own citizens – leaving the bodies of mothers huddled over their dead children. This is a regime that agreed to international inspections – then kicked out the inspectors. This is a regime that has something to hide from the civilized world.

States like these, and their terrorist allies, constitute an axis of evil, arming to threaten the peace of the world. By seeking weapons of mass destruction, these regimes pose a grave and growing danger. They could provide these arms to terrorists, giving them the means to match their hatred. They could attack our allies or attempt to blackmail the United States. In any of these cases, the price of indifference would be catastrophic.

Our war on terror is well begun, but it is only begun. This campaign may not be finished on our watch – yet it must be and it will be waged on our watch...

"RESOLUTION 1441"
Kofi Annan

On February 8, 2003 little over a month before the US-led coalition invaded Iraq, UN Secretary General Kofi Annan spoke to students at the College of William and Mary, Williamsburg, Virginia, on the ideals of the founders of the United Nations, his vision of its role in the early 21st century and his fears for world security if states decided independently to police the world.

...our founders were not pacifists. They knew there would be times when force must be met with force. And therefore they wrote into the Charter of the United Nations strong enforcement provisions, to enable the world community to unite against aggression and defeat it.

Twelve years ago, when Iraq invaded Kuwait, the Security Council and the United Nations did just that. First the Security Council gave the invader a clear alternative of peaceful withdrawal. Then, when he rejected that offer, the Council authorized the use of force...

This is an issue not for any State alone, but for the international community as a whole. When States decide to use force, not in self- defence but to deal with broader threats to international peace and security, there is no substitute for the unique legitimacy provided by the United Nations Security Council. States and peoples around the world attach fundamental importance to such legitimacy, and to the international rule of law....Only a collective, multilateral approach can effectively curb the proliferation of weapons of mass destruction, and make the world a safer place.

Just three months ago the Security Council adopted Resolution 1441, giving a new, more authoritative and robust mandate to the United Nations weapons inspectors in Iraq. This resolution was negotiated with patience and persistence, and as a result was adopted unanimously. That gives it even greater authority – an authority based on law, collective effort and the unique legitimacy of the United Nations. This was multilateral diplomacy at its best, serving the cause of peace and security.

If the Council stands united – as it did in adopting Resolution 1441 – it will have a greater impact, and a better chance of achieving its objective, which must be a comprehensive solution that brings the Iraqi people, who have suffered so much, fully back into the international community...

That is important because what happens in Iraq does not take place in a vacuum. It has implications – for better or worse – for other issues of great importance to the United States, and to the world. For instance, it will greatly affect the climate in which we conduct our struggle against international terrorism.

The broader our consensus on Iraq, the better the chance that we can come together again and deal effectively with other burning conflicts in the world, which you heard recited earlier this morning...When there is strong US leadership, exercised through patient diplomatic persuasion and coalition-building, the United Nations is successful – and the United States is successful. The United Nations is most useful to all its members, including the United States, when it is united, and works as a source of collective action rather than discord.

I ask all Americans present to keep this in mind – and especially you, the students of this great college, with its long tradition of community service. Many of you are about to choose your career. I hope a good number of you will go into the public service. You may not earn much, but you will be happy and fulfilled. But I hope all of you, whatever your profession, will be seeking to serve the public, and to contribute to the welfare not only of your country but of all your fellow human beings – especially those who live in poverty and misery on other continents, and yearn for lives free from want, and free from fear.

"REASONS FOR INVADING IRAQ"
Tony Blair

On March 18, 2003, the British parliament debated the imminent invasion of Iraq. Less than 36 hours after the debate ended the first explosions were heard in Baghdad.

...the outcome of this issue will now determine more than the fate of the Iraqi regime and more than the future of the Iraqi people, for so long brutalized by Saddam. It will determine the way Britain and the world confront the central security threat of the 21st century; the development of the UN; the relationship between Europe and the US; the relations within the EU and the way the US engages with the rest of the world...

We are now seriously asked to accept that in the last few years, contrary to all history, contrary to all intelligence, he decided unilaterally to destroy the weapons. Such a claim is palpably absurd...Iraq continues to deny it has any WMD, though no serious intelligence service anywhere in the world believes them....

The only persuasive power to which he responds is 250,000 allied troops on his doorstep....

The way ahead was so clear. It was for the UN to pass a second Resolution setting out benchmarks for compliance; with an ultimatum that if they were ignored, action would follow.

The tragedy is that had such a Resolution been issued, he might just have complied. Because the only route to peace with someone like Saddam Hussein is diplomacy backed by force...

Our fault has not been impatience...The truth is our patience should have been exhausted weeks and months and years ago. Even now – when if the world united and gave him an ultimatum:

comply or face forcible disarmament he might just do it – the world hesitates and in that hesitation he senses weakness and therefore continues to defy.

What would any tyrannical regime possessing WMD think viewing the history of the world's diplomatic dance with Saddam? That our capacity to pass firm resolutions is matched only by our feebleness in implementing them.

That is why this indulgence has to stop. Because it is dangerous. It is dangerous if such regimes disbelieve us. Dangerous if they think they can use our weakness, our hesitation, even the natural urges of our democracy towards peace, against us. Dangerous because one day they will mistake our innate revulsion against war for permanent incapacity; when in fact, pushed to the limit, we will act...

But, of course, in a sense, any fair observer does not really dispute that Iraq is in breach and that 1441 implies action in such circumstances. The real problem is that, underneath, people dispute that Iraq is a threat; dispute the link between terrorism and WMD; dispute the whole basis of our assertion that the two together constitute a fundamental assault on our way of life...

I have come to the conclusion after much reluctance that the greater danger to the UN is inaction: that to pass Resolution 1441 and then refuse to enforce it would do the most deadly damage to the UN's future strength, confirming it as an instrument of diplomacy but not of action, forcing nations down the very unilateralist path we wish to avoid.

...And the moment that a new government is in place, willing to disarm Iraq of WMD, for which its people have no need or purpose - then let sanctions be lifted in their entirety.

I have never put our justification for action as regime change. We have to act within the terms set out in Resolution 1441. That is our legal base...

Index

Acknowledgements

"The Ten Commandments" – The Bible (King James Version), Exodus 20:1-17. Crown Copyright.

"Christian Love" – The Bible (New International Version), I Corinthians, 13 4–7. Crown Copyright.

"Greater Love Hath No Man" – The Bible (King James Version), John 15:9-17. Crown Copyright

"The Sermon on the Mount" – The Bible (King James Version), Mathew 5:1–7:27. Crown Copyright

Neville Chamberlain – Crown copyright

Winston Churchill – Estate of Sir Winston S. Churchill, c/o Curtis Brown Literary Agency, London.

James Crick and Francis Watson, originally published in *Nature* magazine.

Vaclav Havel, from *Open Letters: Selected Writings* 1965-1990 by Vaclav Havel, translated by Paul Wilson, copyright © 1991 by A.G. Brain. Preface/translation copyright © 1985, 1988, 1991 by Paul Wilson. Used by permission of Alfred A. Knopf, a division of Random House, Inc.

Dalai Lama, from *The Art of Happiness*, His Holiness the Dalai Lama and Howard C. Culter, reproduced by permission of Hodder and Stoughton Ltd.

Martin Luther King, estate of Martin Luther King, Jnr, c/o Writers House, New York.

John F. Kennedy – by permission of John Fitzgerald Kennedy Library/NARA

Nelson Mandela – by permission of the Nelson Mandela Foundation

Pope John Paul II, "Our Lady of Jasna Góra", courtesy of the Catholic Truth Society

Franklin D. Roosevelt – Courtesy Franklin Digital Archives/NARA

Harry S. Truman – Courtesy Harry S. Truman Presidential Library/NARA

Ian Wilmut, "Dolly the Sheep" – Text of speech copyright the Roslin Institute, Edinburgh

Tony Blair – Parliamentary copyright material is reproduced with permission of the Controller of Her Majesty's Stationery Office on behalf of Parliament.

"I Have a Dream" – Reprinted by arrangement with the Estate of Martin Luther King Jr., c/o Writers House as agent for the proprietor New York, NY. Copyright 1963 Martin Luther King Jr., copyright renewed 1991 Coretta Scott King.

"Stride Toward Freedom" – Reprinted by arrangement with the Estate of Martin Luther King Jr., c/o Writers House as agent for the proprietor New York, NY. Copyright 1958 Martin Luther King Jr., copyright renewed 1986 Coretta Scott King.